LINER

Fifty years of passenger ship photographs

LINER

Fifty years of passenger ship photographs

William H. Miller

Patrick Stephens, Wellingborough

To Everett Viez
for his skill and thoughtfulness in creating
and collecting many of the photographs in these pages

© Bill Miller 1986

2 4 6 8 10 9 7 5 3

British Library Cataloguing in Publication Data

Miller, William H.
Liner.
1. Ocean liners———History
I. Title
387.2'432'0904   HE566.025

ISBN 0-85059-765-X

*Patrick Stephens Limited is part of the
Thorsons Publishing Group*

Printed in Great Britain
by Butler & Tanner Ltd, Frome and London

Contents

In special dedication to Her Majesty Queen Elizabeth, the Queen Mother who named the Queen Elizabeth, Strathmore, Windsor Castle *and* Northern Star, *among others, and who sailed in both Cunard 'Queens'. Her Majesty is shown aboard the* Queen Elizabeth 2, *in December 1982, receiving the staff and servicemen who sailed with the liner to the South Atlantic.* (Southern Newspapers plc.)

Introduction

While writing and organizing this book in the winter of 1984-85, interest in the great liners seems to have reached a new peak. It is perhaps quite fitting that this work begins with the debut of the *Normandie*, the most magnificent of all liners. It has been fifty years since she first appeared on the North Atlantic run. A travelling exhibit was staged in France, heralding the anniversary. Several of the ship's grand salon panels went on exhibit in the lobby of a New York City skyscraper, a 50 in long wood model of the ship went on auction for $500 and one of her brass steam whistles, used since the mid forties at a steel plant in Pennsylvania, was ceremoniously given over to the Ocean Liner Museum Project. The memory of the *Normandie*, a ship which sailed only for just over four years and then after a long lay-up burned at her New York pier, typifies the intrigue and curiosity with the great age of the ocean liner.

Mostly in pictures, this book is an attempt to follow the extraordinary changes which passenger shipping has withstood over this past half-century. The glory, the one-upmanship and even the unprofitability of the mid and late thirties (just as the biggest, fastest and grandest ships of all time sailed into service) led to those hideously destructive years of the Second World War. It is difficult to comprehend that only two of the pre-war superships reappeared intact; the *Queen Mary* was returned to her original state while Germany's *Europa* was transformed into France's *Liberté*. Those high-peak days of the thirties would never again be equalled. *Bremen*, *Rex*, *Conte di Savoia* and *Normandie* had met with the wreckers by the late forties while the *Empress of Britain*, the biggest Allied merchant ship to be lost, was well settled in her underwater grave.

Post-war prosperity, the emergence of a new travelling middle class and more tourists than ever, produced a triumphant revival on the North Atlantic. For a decade or so, until the late fifties, it was the most successful financial period in transatlantic history. It was also the last, the blunt end of an era. The commercial jet came (at first in 1958), immediately conquered and eventually sent every ship (and some shippers) to seek out new life in the cruise trades. Many of the liners were actually unable to readapt to warm-weather voyaging and sailed off, with nostalgic newspaper reports, crowds along the quayside and fireboat sprays, to distant scrapyards. The sounds of throaty whistles, of band music on deck and creaking panels in the main lounge were replaced by the echoes of hammers and drills from the scrap crews aboard a lonely *Ile de France* at Osaka, the *Liberté* at La Spezia, *Mauretania* at Inverkeithing and *Queen Elizabeth*, after her devastating fiery end, at Hong Kong. By the mid seventies, with the exception of Cunard's *Queen Elizabeth 2* and Poland's little *Stefan Batory*, the transatlantic fleet—that sixty or so ships that sailed since 1945—were gone completely.

On the more extensive, long-distance trades—to Latin America, South Africa, Australia and the Far East—the older pre-war ships were joined by fresh post-war additions. Reaching a peak in the fifties, supported by colonial links, immense movements of migrants and government personnel, a new tourist trade and important, steady flows of cargo, these ships were equally affected by a series of disruptive blows. While the jet appeared somewhat later as a serious competitor, the break-up of the colonial trades had already eliminated some of these ships. Then there was the transition to the container era meaning that cargoes went to far larger, faster and more efficient vessels. In the very end the economics had become crucial; fuel, labour and general operation expenses were such that many of these ships, even when filled to the last berth in tourist or third class, were unable to break even. The last of their kind, loyal sea-going travellers found, by the seventies, that it was no longer convenient or even possible to sail to Rio, Durban, Auckland or Kobe.

The current generation of cruiseships is, however, the link to these earlier ships. The £3 billion ($4 billion)* cruise industry in the United States may well lead to the biggest passenger ship ever, a 200,000-tonner with space for 4-5,000 passengers. She would cost £390 million ($500 million). Ironically, while there are fewer passenger ships in service at present (1985) than, say, thirty or fifty years ago, more travellers are in fact going by sea than ever before. The leisure cruise industry, with its exceptionally comfortable, well-fed and well-entertained ships, has lured more and more vacationers to the seas of the Caribbean, the Aegean, the Baltic and even the far off South Pacific.

While the *Normandie* and her generation are gone, and while the *Queen Mary* serves as a monument to that earlier era in her Southern California retirement, the photographs in this book are intended to portray the exceptional change that the ocean liner has withstood. The evolution will continue.

William H. Miller
Jersey City, New Jersey, Spring 1985

*Please note that throughout this book conversions between pounds sterling and US dollars have been calculated according to the average exchange rate for the year in question.

Acknowledgements

Many most kind and helpful individuals have been involved in the creation of this book. Finding high quality, unpublished photographs of passenger liners, both large and small, has become increasingly difficult. Therefore, I am especially grateful to the spectacular assistance of Everett Viez, one of the foremost collectors of ocean liner photos in the world. Without ever having met me, he forwarded from his home in Florida a superb grouping of unseen liner views. Without his assistance, this book would not have been possible. Additional important help came from Frank Braynard's giant files, from the Hapag-Lloyd and from Hapag-Lloyd Shipyards, from Stephen Rabson at the P&O Group Library in London and from Goran Damstrom, the manager of technical information at the Wartsila Shipyards at Helsinki.

I am also especially indebted to the most gracious and skilled support from Luis Miguel Correia, a highly capable marine photographer at Lisbon; John Havers, who has a priceless photo collection in bound albums; Richard K. Morse, who owns one of the greatest photo collections in New York City; Hisashi Noma in Japan; Thomas Young at the Port Authority of New York & New Jersey; Victor Scrivens and his finely catalogued photo files in Coral Gables, Florida; and the Southern Newspapers at Southampton.

Other assistance came from Marius Bar, J. K. Byass, Fred Hawks, R. Izawa, Robert Lenzer, Fred Rodriguez, Captain Robert Russell, Roger Sherlock, Willie Tinnemeyer and Barry Winiker. Firms which offered help include the Cunard Line, Europe-Canada Line, French Line, Holland-America Line, Home Lines, Moore-McCormack Lines, Moran Towing & Transportation Company, the Nedlloyd Group, Newport News Shipbuilding & Drydock Company, Operation Mobilisation, the Solent News Agency, Todd Shipyards and the Union-Castle Line.

Chapter 1

Superships of the thirties

On 3 June 1935 the French liner *Normandie* reached New York for the first time. It was the most spectacular maiden voyage of all. Not only had the ship, the first of the 'thousand-footers', captured the Blue Riband taking it from the Italian *Rex*, but it was the formal introduction of the most glamorous and sumptuous liner ever built. No passenger ship, superliner or otherwise, has had quite the same impact as the exquisite *Normandie*. One reporter described her gala reception in New York Harbor as:

"*Normandie* Wins Blue Riband!" This was how newspapers and maritime bulletins, from the North River to the Seine, headlined the arrival of the French Line's new superliner after her maiden crossing. On May 5th, the day the huge vessel sailed away from the St Nazaire-Penhoet shipyards, where she had been painstakingly built, everyone from her designers to the humblest workman in the yard was already saying that here was a grand enfant destined for greatness. When her French Line predecessor, the *Ile de France*, went into service in 1927, the Compagnie Générale Transatlantique was already planning for the *Normandie*. "She shall be the finest ship ever launched", was their resolve. Her accommodations and decorations were such that the most refined concepts of modern comfort and luxury could be satisfied. Those close to the great ship in her earliest days were fond of saying, "The *Normandie* has been designed as a floating embassy of France itself."

'After her speed trials from the Glenans base, bright hopes became established fact. The huge ship, over 1,000 ft long, was indeed the world's fastest passenger liner. A few weeks later, the *Normandie* was enthusiastically welcomed in New York. On this first voyage, the ocean greyhound crossed the Atlantic from Bishop's Rock to Ambrose Light in just four days, three hours and fourteen minutes. The news of the record preceded her. As the *Normandie* entered Upper New York Bay, flying from her masthead an azure pennant a yard long for each knot cut from the transatlantic mark she had just broken, greeting airplanes and dirigibles, tugs, freighters and excursion boats tooted wildly in welcome, and fireboats spouted pyramids of water in celebration. According to some harbor masters, she was escorted to her pier by the largest and noisiest fleets of small craft ever to take part in such a demonstration in the busy waters of New York.'

The *Normandie* was the French entry into the superliner sweepstakes of the thirties. In almost all ways, she was the superior ship. The Germans started this, the greatest and last serious competition among the liner nations of Europe, in 1929 with their speedy near-sisters *Bremen* and *Europa*. The *Bremen* blatantly snatched the Blue Riband from Britain's *Mauretania*, an illustrious four-stacker that had held the title for 22 years. Soon afterwards, the *Europa* took the trophy from her sister. While it was very important to have the world's largest ship (or at least the longest) or alternately the most luxurious or best-fed, absolutely nothing was quite as prestigious or supposedly secured more passengers than the Blue Riband. There was an enormous thrill for many Atlantic travellers to send postcard greetings from 'the world's fastest ship'.

The *Normandie* and an equally large and powerful new Cunarder were designed as the first thousand-footers, the ultimate generation of superships. Almost everything about them was in the superlative. They had great size, power and luxury, and another highly desirable quality, the consistent ability to stay in the headlines. After all, to a considerable extent they were created as large centrepieces of public relations. Considering that the Depression had started almost just as their constructions began in the shipyards, the grim forecasts on the future of passenger shipping, especially on the declining North Atlantic and particularly for such excessively expensive big ships, they might never have been. There were certainly rumours that both ships would be scrapped and abandoned when little more than steel shells. There was even talk that Cunard, in a highly secret proposal to the French, would cancel their new liner if the same was done with the *Normandie*. However, while not all board members were confident that trading conditions on the North Atlantic would improve, government ministers in both London and Paris advanced moneys to complete the ships with a more attainable intention; national goodwill. What better ambassador could the French have, for example, than a technologically advanced and decoratively stunning flagship. If the earlier *Ile de France* had won high praises, the *Normandie*'s impressions and influence would be incalculable. And so these supportive Parisian ministers glowed with satisfaction as the liner made news almost everywhere and then established a legendary reputation that exceeded the wildest dreams of the French Line's press offices. Certainly the ship of the thirties, she is—even at this distance in time, a half century since her delivery —the very pinnacle of ocean liner creation and development. While the British spent some £7.3 million ($36 million) on their new liner (they would build an equally priced running-mate as well), the French seemed to have no limits and finished up with a £12 million ($60 million) price tag for the *Normandie*. Much of the additional money went into the decoration.

Author John Malcolm Brinnin, in his *The Sway of the Grand Saloon*, wrote: 'In the album of vanished Atlantic liners, the *Normandie* figures as a ship without peer. Probably, the greatest ship built anywhere, she was a lively and beloved legend while she lived. All in all, the result, to most Frenchmen, was overwhelming. To a question posed by one of the proudest of them —"What palace, what Triumphal Way, what memorial have we built to perpetuate our civilization, as the cathedrals perpetuate that of the Middle Ages, the castles of the Loire that of the Renaissance, and Versailles that of the age of Louix XIV?"—the only answer was

"The *Normandie*!" '

The designers and decorators of the *Normandie* made the most exceptional uses of space and material, stunning creations in all that had never been seen before on the high seas. She was the ultimate height of ocean liner style, assuredly pre-war moderne. The *Ile de France*, thought to be a preliminary to the new supership, was well surpassed.

The *Normandie*'s first class dining room was one of her finest creations. With its heavily coffered ceilings and strongly articulated beams, the room was a high revival of the intent of empire; to create a sense of strong, national wealth. Like the new Cunarder and others, one of the *Normandie*'s intentions was to suggest, at least to the outside world, that France was, in fact, gloriously surviving the otherwise sinister Depression. The restaurant was boldly advertised as being slightly larger than the Hall of Mirrors at Versailles. It measured some 300 ft in length, rose three full decks in height and sat 1,000 guests at over 400 tables. The fountain-like lighting fixtures were of specially created Lalique while other materials included bronze and hammered glass. Two huge bronze doors opened in the dining room, each boasting five medallions from Norman cities, including the ship's home port of Le Havre. (These medallions were removed in the early stages of her wartime conversion to a troop transport, placed in storage and then—through the extreme generosity of a wealthy parishioner—found their way to Our Lady of Lebanon Church in Brooklyn Heights, New York.)

Dining was a legend aboard the French liners. They were thought by legions of Atlantic travellers to be the best-fed ships on the North Atlantic run, a distinction best exemplified by the advertising slogan 'More seagulls follow the *Paris* [an earlier French liner from 1921] than any other ship, all in hopes of catching some scraps of food!' Aboard the *Normandie*, as with all else about her, there seemed to be no limits. The underlining notion in planning and creating was to be extreme, all extravagant and outrageous. A sample dinner menu aboard the new flagship might include seven items for hors d'oeuvre, five soups, pike in butter sauce and fillets of turbot for the fish course, braised sweetbreads for an entrée, a special French recipe of Duckling à l'Orange, three vegetables, five kinds of potato, four pastas, two roasts, nine items from the cold buffet, six salad choices, six cheeses, two French pastries, three puddings, five flavours of ice cream, two fresh fruits, two wines (which were free of charge, as aboard all of the French liners) and finally assorted coffees and teas.

The ship's Grand Salon, also decorated with original Lalique and hand-woven tapestries and offset by gilded columns, was a centrepiece of social life onboard. The Winter Garden, which had a tropical setting of exotic greenery and bubbling fountains, also included caged birds. The Grill Room, which doubled as the ship's nightclub, was surrounded by large windows, which gave it a particular sunny flavour during the day. By night, the mood became subdued, almost seductive, with draped windows and dimmed iridescent lighting. Dance music filled the air. The indoor pool, done in intricate mosaic tiles, consisted of 80 ft of graduated levels. In addition to the customary gift shops, there was a florist, a special gardener, a clothing and even a chocolate shop. The staterooms, especially in first class, were wonders among themselves. All of the first class rooms were done in a different style or decor. The Caen Suite, for example, which was second only to the penthouses named Deauville and Trouville, consisted of a separate living room, private dining room (with an adjacent warming kitchen), four bedrooms, four bathrooms and trunk room. In the late thirties, when the *Normandie* was sent on two exceptional 'Carnival in Rio' cruises from New York, fares in this suite for the three-week voyage were listed as £1,840 ($9,200) for each of eight occupants.

The *Normandie* had settled into service for slightly less than a year when her most serious (and superior) rival appeared. Cunard had hoped to deliver their new giant in 1933 or even 1934, but at least in advance of the French ship. Ordered from the famous John Brown Shipyards on the Clyde, where the earlier *Lusitania* and *Aquitania* among others had been built, her first keel plates were laid down in December 1930. A year later, with little more than the 1,018 ft steel shell in place, construction came to a screeching halt. The sinister Depression, causing drastic declines on the North Atlantic run and prompting the Cunard Company's first major financial losses, put the entire project in a sensitive limbo. Some thought she should be abandoned, others that she should be sold 'as is' to a more solid American company while others, in more considered reflection, suggested that the idea should sit out the worrisome years ahead. Work was not restarted for over two years, until the spring of 1934. Consequently, this British flagship would be delayed considerably, appearing well after her French counterpart building at St Nazaire. In

silence, Cunard had to be patient.

The decision to build these enormous superliners—the Germans with their *Bremen* and *Europa*, the Italians with the *Rex* and *Conte di Savoia* and then the French with the *Normandie* and the British with not one but a pair of exceptional express ships—was not all simplicity. Each of them were enormously bold ventures. The Atlantic passenger trade was, and continued to be, one of extreme variables, particularly in the twenties and thirties. The age of the pre-First World War prosperity was gone forever. That steady flow of westbound immigrant traffic to America, which filled the lower deck quarters and therefore guaranteed profits for the likes of the first *Mauretania*, *Olympic*, *Imperator* and even the *Titanic* if she had survived her maiden crossing, had disappeared. In 1914, on the eve of the First World War, over one million people made the journey to American shores—almost all of them in steerage quarters. The marble-clad, potted palm first class, while so often remembered and written of, made far less of a financial contribution to the treasuries of the likes of Cunard, White Star and Hamburg American. It was one of the great ironies of the transatlantic liner trade. However, by 1924 the immigrant trade had slumped to a scant 150,000, a result largely of the strict American immigration quotas of 1921. The liners, having lost their most important bloodlines of support, created new, refined, more comfortable third class (later tourist class) spaces for budget tourists, students and teachers, and most especially the rising American middle classes. Those bare steel bunks and almost sinister dormitories of steerage were replaced by cabins with attendant stewards and an overall sense of comfort, cleanliness and ample ventilation.

In the twenties liners such as the Cunarders and the French ships carried three classes of passenger; first, second and third. The former was realistically as opulent and as comfortable as any description has ever suggested. There were vast and sumptuous lounges, soft chairs and enormous fireplaces, columned restaurants with elaborate menus, secluded grill rooms, apartment-like suites, private terraces and even thoughtfully placed adjoining quarters for personal servants. In that era, long before commercial transoceanic aircraft, first class rosters included lists of the famous and near-famous; Mary Pickford and Douglas Fairbanks, F. Scott Fitzgerald, Will Rogers, Gertrude Stein, Charlie Chaplin, Queen Marie of Rumania, Rudolf Valentino, Sir Thomas Lipton, the Crown

Prince of Sweden and the Grand Duchess of Russia, and those names of American corporate royalty such as Astor, Guggenheim, Morgan and Vanderbilt. Even the enormously popular Prince of Wales, later Edward VIII and then the Duke of Windsor, crossed to New York aboard Cunard's *Berengaria* in 1924, but disguised rather thinly as Lord Renfrew. He fooled no one. Instead, he sensibly abandoned his seclusion and took brisk strolls along the boat deck, joined in a tug o'war and danced well into the small hours in the main ballroom. The rich, famous and celebrated were prized clientele. Every effort was made by steamer companies to attract and then retain their loyalty. The most certain technique was to have the newest, largest and—most preferably—the fastest liner.

The second class accommodation was a refinement of first class, although with far less obvious glitter, space and even less effort on the part of the hotel staff to 'bend and please.' Menus offered less of a selection and service tended to be not quite as prompt. However, it was a highly popular mode of travel. In later years, when second class became a more comfortable cabin class, Cunard aptly called it 'the happy medium'. Such middle-priced accommodation lacked the starched stuffiness of first class yet had more space, entertainment and even a better sense of fun than third or tourist class. One traveller in the twenties suggested that the very best way to travel the Atlantic by liner was 'at third class rates, but in second class quarters.' The barriers between those two lower shipboard classes were far more easily transcended. A remote passageway or door led 'upwards' to a better world. Years later, aboard the two-class *France* of 1961, some tourist passengers found that the chapel was, in fact, the easiest entry into first class. However, slipping into first class, no matter how discreetly, was no easy feat. I recall during a crossing from Naples to New York in as late as 1973, aboard the Italian *Raffaello*, how stewards who suspected passengers of having transcended between the ship's three classes would rather discreetly ask for their restaurant table numbers. It seemed that the numbering sequences were quite different for each of the three restaurants.

By 1931, newer and faster superliners were gaining in popularity, if only momentarily. Germany's brand new *Europa*, the latest Blue Riband champion, carried over 43,000 passengers that year while her near-sister *Bremen*, just a year older and just having lost the Blue Riband, averaged 42,000. (By the mid thirties, however, this German pair would be less popular and suc-

cessful, primarily due to the anti-Nazi sentiment that was then growing.) Older big ships such as Cunard's express trio on the other hand, had fallen from favour—and on hard times. The *Aquitania* (from 1914) carried nearly 22,000 passengers while the *Berengaria* averaged 13,500 and the *Mauretania* fell into last place with a scant 12,500. In the face of such figures and future trends, creating a new flagship of over 80,000 tons and with 2,000 berths was a sizeable gamble.

Any worries Cunard might have had, however, were well displaced soon after the new Cunarder's first appearance in the late spring of 1936. Following considerable rumour and part truths that said she would be named *Victoria*, the new national flagship was launched as the *Queen Mary* in September 1934 and later embarked on the most successful career of all the big superships. While briefly the world's largest liner (within months, the French *Normandie* had extensions added to her aft decks which pushed her overall tonnage to 83,000, compared to the *Queen Mary*'s 81,000) and while the Cunarder later secured the Blue Riband permanently, the *Queen Mary* was a more conservative ship in many ways. Certainly, her appearance—which was based largely on a refinement of the old four-stacker *Aquitania* and therefore made little obvious concession to the mid thirties age of streamlining—inspired a warm appeal. The beautiful *Normandie*, which was far less successful in luring passengers (she averaged a mere 57 per cent occupancy rate for one season), might have appeared to be 'too' modern, in the way that a spaceship might be contrasted to a Boeing 747. The *Normandie*'s glittering, high style interiors, while sumptuous to almost everyone who saw them, inhibited many prospective travellers. She was, quite simply, far too luxurious for the more ordinary tourists. On the other hand, the *Queen Mary* was done in glossy veneers, stuffed chairs and sofas, fireplaces and with that unmistakable quality of being both a British ship and a Cunarder. She established a far better rapport and reputation with the general tourist trade.

It should not be inferred that the French were unhappy with the *Normandie*. She achieved magnificently in all ways, except in financial profit, the original intentions of her designers, owners and government sponsors. In the late thirties serious consideration was well under way toward building an even larger, more powerful and more extravagant version of her, supposedly to be called *Bretagne*. In *Damned by Destiny*, authors David L. Williams and Richard

P. De Kerbrech wrote that the 'Bretagne project' might have begun in the autumn of 1939, with launching in the autumn of 1942 and then commissioning in the spring of 1944. She would be the ideal high speed running mate to the *Normandie* and would thereby allow the French to run a weekly service in each direction, between Le Havre, Southampton and New York. Previously, the *Normandie* ran an independent schedule, which was always a disappointment, and was assisted erratically by such slower ships as the *Ile de France, Champlain, Lafayette* and *Paris*. Among other reasons, the *Bretagne* was abandoned due to the sudden eruption of the Second World War. Afterwards, however, in 1945–46, the *Normandie*'s designer, a Russian emigrant named Vladimir Yourkevitch, proposed a pair of 'super French liners that would be 100,000 tons and 1,148 ft in length compared to their predecessor's 82,000 tons and 1,029 ft. This idea, however, never came to pass.

Just months before the *Queen Mary*'s maiden departure in May 1936, Cunard announced their plans for a second supership, the partner of their well-planned two-ship express service, which was to begin in April 1940. This new liner was not a sistership, but reflected more modern and contemporary ideas. She would have twin instead of triple funnels, cleaner upper decks, a sharper rake in her bow and even a more spacious 'flow' in her accommodation. Whereas the *Queen Mary* was a groundbreaking ship for her time, in the early thirties, this second liner—which would be named as the *Queen Elizabeth* during her launching in September 1938—had the exceptional benefits of using ideas not only from her Cunard predecessor, but from the German and Italian giants as well as, and most significantly, from the brilliant *Normandie*. Although she would never quite have the same extraordinary sparkle that belonged to the *Queen Mary*, the *Queen Elizabeth* finally entered service, after strenuous wartime duties, in the autumn of 1946 and thereafter set out on a most successful career. While statistically the largest liner ever created, at 83,600 tons and 1,031 ft in length, she never officially attempted to take the Blue Riband, an honour which Cunard wisely left to the *Queen Mary* alone.

The Queens, especially in later years, were always warm and comfortable ships, with appealing homely qualities, even despite their three-deck-high lounges and restaurants, chromium-filled verandah bars and glossy shopping arcades. An advertisement from 1936 hints at their unique atmosphere and attitude toward ocean travel:

'A ship becomes the centre of the universe. . . today as when sailing ships were uncharted points on the blue of the globe. The men on the bridge of a modern liner know that destiny is in their hands as inexorably as it ever was. They check their bearings still by sun, moon and stars. The size of their ship only multiplies their responsibility. . . makes more vital, more valuable the stern tradition of Britain on the seas.

'Passengers, too, feel this unique position. . . isolated and yet a focal point of all the world. To this is due the special congeniality of shipboard life. . . and the opportunity to make that life something nearer to perfection than can be found ashore. For all time this has been true, and for nearly one hundred years Cunard-White Star has been approaching that perfection. It can, of course, only be achieved by the efforts of men and women. . . however huge a ship may be. It's still the men that count. . . the British tradition distinguishes Cunard-White Star.

'November sailings are delightful. . . the next crossings to the British Isles and the Continent are:

Queen Mary	November 4th
Scythia	November 7th
Aquitania	November 11th
Carinthia	November 14th
Queen Mary	November 18th
Laconia	November 21st
Berengaria	November 25th
Samaria	November 27th'

It was this prevailing sense of strong tradition, seamanship and superb service which made the Cunarders, particularly the *Queen Mary*, among the most successful Atlantic liners of the late thirties.

The two Germans, the *Bremen* and *Europa*, were marvels in their time in the late twenties. They were first designed as 35,000-tonners, modified versions of the North German Lloyd's flagship *Columbus*. But, as Germany recovered further from the devastation of the First World War, the ideas of surpassing British maritime might resurfaced. They had been successful in 1897 when their *Kaiser Wilhelm der Grosse*, the first of the four-stackers, took the Blue Riband from Cunard's *Lucania*. Fifteen years later they produced the biggest liner of all at the time, the 52,000-ton, 4,700-passenger *Imperator*, which was, in fact, the first of a successively larger trio. Ironically the third of these, the 56,000-ton *Bismarck*, never sailed for her German owners, but was given over to the British after the hostilities and then became the world's largest liner, White Star's *Majestic*, under British colours.

The *Bremen* and *Europa* were the new post-war contenders for transatlantic honours. Redesigned in the early stages of construction, with more powerful engines and reaching some 50,000 tons each, the new team gave the Germans such confidence that they even planned simultaneous maiden crossings for both ships to take the Blue Riband from Cunard's *Mauretania*. In fact, the *Europa* suffered a serious shipyard fire and was delayed by a year, so the *Bremen* took the pennant singlehandedly in her maiden summer of 1929. The British would not regain the trophy permanently for nearly a decade, until 1938.

John Malcolm Brinnin described the *Bremen* as the appropriate 'sea monster' that she was: 'Even at a glance the *Bremen* communicated excitement of something arrestingly novel and genuinely new. Her hull, constructed on an oval plan, had lines that gave her an air of graceful staunchness; her two massive funnels were stocky and short, getting away completely from that somewhat precarious stovepipe feeling that characterized the pre-war liners. They were in fact too short, almost stubby. Though they conveyed a sense of potency, they also conveyed splashes of oil and smut that made her open decks aft a hazard for promenaders and passengers bundled in deckchairs. But even when these were replaced, the *Bremen*'s big stacks were still notably shorter than those of any other big ship. Her two masts were raked back like the funnels with military smartness. A suggestion of streamlining emanated from her rounded-off bridge. Her breadth of 102 ft made her the broadest ship on the ocean and, to one observer, gave her the appearance of a "vast seagoing cathedral of steel".'

The *Bremen* and *Europa* travelled the same northern course, between the Channel ports and New York, and with the obvious extension to Bremerhaven as well, that rivalled the established superliners of the time, Cunard's 'Big Three' of *Aquitania, Berengaria* and *Mauretania* and White Star's *Majestic, Olympic* and *Homeric*. They prompted shipping directors in London, Liverpool and Paris, among other corporate seats, to think of new tonnage, larger, more powerful and assuredly more magnificent creations. The Germans, in fact, started the great supership race of the thirties, the last of its kind in such overwhelming numbers and statistics.

Italy, under the Mussolini regime, responded with two supership projects of their own, certainly bids at transatlantic recordbreaking, but for a far less established service, on the southern route out of the Mediterranean. While designed as separate ships for different companies, the Navigazione Generale Italiana and the Lloyd Sabaudo, they were brought together as a team when Mussolini ordered that all Italian passenger lines be merged for efficiency and effectiveness. Consequently, the 51,000-ton *Rex* and the 48,000-ton *Conte di Savoia*, both of 1932, signalled the emergence of a new name on the transatlantic run, the Italian Line.

The *Rex* achieved maritime immortality when she took the Blue Riband from the Germans, in 1933. It went two years later to the *Normandie*. Otherwise, the two ships were glorious symbols of Italian design and decoration, 'floating palazzi' as one historian described them, but were far too big for those early days on the Mediterranean route. Most passengers still used the northern passage, even those bound for Mediterranean destinations, who would travel by train from Le Havre or Cherbourg. The *Rex* and *Conte di Savoia*, dubbed as the 'Rivieras afloat' with sand scattered about their upper lido decks, were again profitable in prestige but little else.

The enthusiasm for big ships spread to others as well. Canadian Pacific built their largest liner of all, the 42,300-ton *Empress of Britain*, for the St Lawrence trade between Southampton and Quebec City, and then de luxe winter world cruising. The Dutch built a new national flagship, the first major ship in one of their own dockyards, which was commissioned as the *Nieuw Amsterdam* in 1938.

The largest liners afloat in 1935–36 made an impressive list:

	Tonnage	Length	Passengers	Flag
Normandie	82,800	1,028 ft	1,972	French
Queen Mary	81,200	1,018 ft	1,957	British
Leviathan	59,900	950 ft	3,008	American
Majestic	56,500	956 ft	2,145	British
Berengaria	52,200	919 ft	2,722	British
Bremen	51,600	938 ft	2,231	German
Rex	51,000	879 ft	2,032	Italian
Europa	49,700	936 ft	2,244	German
Conte di Savoia	48,500	814 ft	2,060	Italian
Olympic	46,400	882 ft	2,021	British
Aquitania	45,600	901 ft	1,789	British
Ile de France	43,100	791 ft	1,262	French
L'Atlantique	42,500	742 ft	1,156	French

	Tonnage	Length	Passengers	Flag
Empress of Britain	42,300	758 ft	1,195	British
Paris	34,500	763 ft	912	French
Homeric	34,300	776 ft	1,378	British
Augustus	32,600	711 ft	2,210	Italian
Roma	32,500	709 ft	1,675	Italian
Columbus	32,300	775 ft	1,724	German
Mauretania	30,700	790 ft	2,165	British
Statendam	29,500	698 ft	1,654	Dutch
Georgic	27,700	711 ft	1,542	British
Cap Arcona	27,500	676 ft	1,315	German
Belgenland	27,100	697 ft	2,600	British
Britannic	26,900	712 ft	1,554	British
Athlone Castle	25,500	725 ft	784	British
Stirling Castle	25,500	725 ft	784	British

Many of the aforementioned ships were, however, victims of the cruel Depression. The *Majestic* and *Olympic*, owned by the financially ailing White Star Line, which was merged with the stronger Cunard Company in 1934, appeared often in their final years scarred in rust. The *Majestic* was sent off her once prestigious run to Southampton for inexpensive cruises to Bermuda while the four-funnel *Olympic*, sistership to the immortal *Titanic*, made £2 ($10) cruises 'to nowhere' and weekend runs from New York to Halifax. A similar fate befell the *Mauretania*, but on more extended trips to ports such as Nassau, Havana and Kingston. On one trip, she carried a mere 175 passengers that were looked after by 600 crew members! The Americans were even harder hit and kept the giant *Leviathan* at her pier for four long, mostly unattended years. She faded with the changing climates, rattled with the alternating currents of the Hudson River and her cold, lonesome innards were looked after by no more than a watchman or two. Most of these ships finished their days in the scrapyards. By 1939, the *Aquitania* was the last survivor of the four-stackers and the sole member of the pre-World War 1 giants.

The remaining superliners continued in service until that fateful late summer of 1939, when almost all commercial services at sea came to an abrupt halt. In the interim years, these ships continued on prescribed patterns, commuting between the Old World and the New. Little boys mostly collected postcards, brochures, booklets and newspaper clippings, often in oversized albums, that recorded these great ships. John Havers, then a teenager along the Southampton Docks, recalled the visits of the major North Atlantic liners in the latter thirties:

'My first visits were to the *Empress of Australia*, that grand three-stacker, onboard which we were given a Nestle's tin of thick milk and a cup of tea [there was no refrigeration aboard many ships at the time]. My enthusiasm soon spread, heightened by a sense of adventure, which included climbing to the crow's nest from inside the foremast.

'A family friend worked for the old Southern Railway, which controlled the docks, and who gave us passes for the tenders out to Cowes Roads [a liner anchorage] to meet the likes of the *Normandie* and the *Bremen*. They also gave us dock passes to board such others as the *Aquitania* and *Berengaria*. I think I spent the whole of the thirties visiting liners. There was so much to see and we wanted to visit everything. I was especially fond of the White Star Line and their ships, and can recall visiting the *Olympic* just as they were testing her steam sirens. They were incredibly similar to those on her sister, the *Titanic*. Alone, the four stacks were an impressive sight. Each was 81½ ft high.

'Visiting other liners, I remember the moose heads in the Smoking Room aboard the *Washington* [United States Lines, 1933]. There was lots of wicker work aboard the old *Rotterdam* [Holland-America Line, 1908]. The *Hansa* [Hamburg American Line, 1923] had a blistered hull for balancing. The big *Bremen* and *Europa* had very dark woods, which appeared somewhat dull after seeing the likes of the *Normandie*. However, both of these giant Germans had exceptional profiles, forerunners to the superb *Nieuw Amsterdam* of 1938. The *Normandie* was, of course, the most exceptional ship. She needed a flotilla of tenders. We would meet more film stars on her tenders than those for any other ship. Onboard, she had the distinctive smell of French cigarettes and expensive perfume. Stepping aboard was a shattering experience. The whole ship seemed to be lacquered gold—gold everywhere—with a great statue on the stairway descending into the restaurant. Alone, the dining room could have held one of the Channel steamers of the day. The floors seemed to be of black marble and fountains of light accentuated the golden furniture. We even visited the inside of the huge third funnel, which was the dog kennel.

'The French Line was very early to experiment with containers for baggage. Great boxes were lifted off railway cars at Southampton, placed aboard the tenders and then hoisted aboard the *Normandie* by one of her cranes and then dropped into the hold. There was never a ship like this one!'

Frank O. Braynard, the well-known American maritime historian and artist, and the curator of the American Merchant Marine Museum, followed the great liners in the thirties as well. As a schoolboy in the early twenties, he is reputed to have been able to spell the name *Leviathan* correctly before he could spell his own name! He has a special fondness for and recollection of the great *Normandie*:

'All through France, in the early fall of 1938, I saw posters inviting people to see the *Normandie* sail on her 100th Atlantic crossing, so I cut my sketching tour of French cathedrals short and went to Le Havre. I found the great French flagship still in drydock and without pass or 'friend in high places' or anything just walked aboard one afternoon. Her wonders were again revealed to me and I spent several hours exploring her rich interiors, finer in my humble opinion than any other liner—ever! The *Leviathan* came a close second. Then, I found a comfortable spot and sat down far aft overlooking the French Line pier and made a detailed pencil sketch of the *Paris*. She was at her pier, the same location where she would burn in April 1939. It was the perfect spot to sketch and when I saw a sailor coming by I gritted my teeth in anticipation of being told to leave. I still had at least 15 minutes more of sketching to do. To my pleasant surprise, the sailor smiled and with great care cleaned the window out of which I was peering, nodding at me as he departed! French courtesy.'

Perhaps New York witnessed the greatest and grandest collections of the great liners, most of them berthed along the specially built West Side piers known as 'Luxury Liner Row.' Three of the terminals, Piers 88, 90 and 92, were built in the mid thirties purposely for the new breed of superliners. The first of these, number 88, was still incomplete when it first received the brand new *Normandie* in the late spring of 1935. Richard K. Morse, an ocean liner historian and devoted collector of memorabilia pertaining to them, has recollections of the Manhattan docks in the late thirties.

'Saturday, January 21st 1939 was a cold, blustery winter day, with occasional snow flurries to spice things up. The greyness of the harbor was relieved only by the colorful smokestacks of the Atlantic liners, docked at their Hudson River piers. At the foot of West 57th Street, we could see the single yellow funnel of the Swedish-American *Drottningholm*, with its characteristic three yellow crowns on a blue disc. Sharing her pier was the *Monarch of Bermuda*, proudly displaying her red-and-black Furness colors. A few blocks south, at 52nd Street, the Italian Line's *Vulcania*, sporting a single short motorship funnel, painted white with a green band and red top, was preparing to depart for the Mediterranean at noon. Next to her, on the north side of Pier 90, was the magnificent *Aquitania*, that beloved old Cunarder proudly flaunting her four orange-and-black stacks and smoking away, preparatory to an 11 am sailing to the Channel ports. Her neighbor, at the French Liner pier [Pier 88], was my most beloved of liners, the *Ile de France*, making ready for an 11:30 am departure, also for England and France. Continuing south, we would encounter the *Columbus* of North German Lloyd, with a 5 pm sailing on a 13-day cruise to the Caribbean. Finally, at West 44th Street, was the *New York*, the Hamburg-American flagship, unloading cargo from the previous day's arrival from Europe. Her light buff-colored stacks with the red-white-black tops contrasted sharply with the plain mustard-colored funnels on the *Columbus*. Of course, the *Ile de France* showed her three deep red-with-black top funnels to complete the palette.

'We paid a dime [10c] apiece to board the *Ile de France* and went up the 'Longest Gangplank in the World,' entering a new world of luxury. The two of us just reveled in the magnificence of the *Ile*'s decor. We visited the main lounge, the first class dining room, the chapel and looked in on a few deluxe staterooms. We wandered all over, mostly in first class, and ended up on the port promenade deck, facing the neighboring Cunard-Wite Star pier. We suddenly heard much triple-chime hooting and, looking upward, saw four huge Cunard funnels moving riverward. The *Aquitania* was on schedule, precisely at 11. It was an unforgettable sight, seeing those big black-and-orange stacks backing out amidst a dreary winter snow flurry. It was time to go ashore; the *Ile de France* was sailing in a half hour.'

More so than any other period in ocean liner history, the thirties were a glittering, opulent, extravagant era. Amidst this final fleet of superliners, there were the biggest, the grandest and the fastest.

France's Normandie *was the most sumptuous, extravagant and noteworthy superliner of her time. She was the highpoint of passenger ship construction and design for the thirties, and possibly for the entire century. She cost an extraordinary £12 million ($60 million), a figure well above the cost of any other equivalent ships, including Britain's* Queen Mary, *which cost £7.3 million ($36 million). Subsidized by the French Government, similar to almost all of the big liners of the time, the* Normandie *was intended to create a record-breaking, luxurious, totally glamorous image for her owners and her nation. The finest designers, decorators, craftsmen and engineers were called to the job. First called the 'super Ile de France', after the celebrated French liner of the mid twenties, the* Normandie *was ordered from the Chantiers de L'Atlantique Shipyard at St Nazaire in 1929. Over a ton of soap, suet and lard were used three years later, on 29 October 1932, when the 1,028 ft long hull first slipped into the waters of the Loire. She was completed, after some Depression-era delays, in the spring of 1935, and then, in May, sped to New York on her record breaking maiden crossing. The commercial history of the most glittering, most impressive, but also one of the most unfortunate superships had begun. She would sail for just over four years. (Robert Russell Collection.)*

It seemed as if all of New York Harbor had turned out to receive the brand new Normandie *in that maiden spring. A small armada of tugs assisted her into Pier 88, still-incomplete, at the foot of West 48th Street in Manhattan. Amidst the overall clutter of her dress flags, she flew the highly prized Blue Riband penant. On her maiden crossing, from Le Havre and Southampton, she had broken the existing record and snatched the honours from Italy's* Rex. *The French liner's run was placed at an average of 32 kt, during a passage time of four days, three hours and fourteen minutes. Among the excited maiden voyage passengers was Madame Lebrun, the First Lady of France. Her French Line owners were delighted with the maiden voyage, the Parisian ministers pleased with their overall investment (and soon gave some thought to an even larger and presumably faster near-sister), but all to the disappointment of the Italians, Germans and mostly to the British, who awaited the completion of their new Riband contender, the* Queen Mary. *(Robert Russell Collection.)*

The Normandie *was a ship of wonders. Thousands came aboard, paying the sum of 50 cents per person, to tour the first class restaurant, which was advertised as being slightly larger than the Hall of Mirrors at Versailles. The walls were done in hammered bronze and glass, and all of the lighting fixtures of specially created Lalique. Equally imposing, the Winter Garden included fresh greenery, flowing fountains and cages of exotic birds. The indoor swimming pool comprised of 80 ft of graduated levels, all done in carefully worked tiles. The ship's best suites, the aptly named Deauville and Trouville, consisted of no less than fifteen interconnecting rooms; bedrooms, bathrooms, closets, trunk rooms, a sitting room, piano salon and even a private dining room and sun deck space.* (Robert Russell Collection.)

In preparation for superliners such as the Normandie *and* Queen Mary, *the first of the 'thousand footers', special provisions had to be made at ports such as Le Havre, Cherbourg, Southampton and New York. Among other problems, the existing Hudson River berths at Manhattan were unsuitable. Consequently, the City commissioned three 'super piers', numbers 88, 90 and 92, and which jutted some 1,100ft from the shoreline. The first of these, number 88, was nearly completed just in time for the* Normandie's *first call, in May 1935.*

In this view taken in March 1937, 'Luxury Liner Row'—as it came to be known—is well occupied. In the lower left is North German Lloyd's Europa, *a 49,700-tonner and Blue Riband champion from 1930; then Italy's 51,000-ton* Rex, *which held the Riband for nearly two years beginning in 1933; then the largest of all, the 82,800-ton* Normandie; *and finally at Cunard White Star's Pier 90, at the foot of West 50th Street, are the 27,000-ton* Georgic *and the 52,000-ton* Berengaria. *(French Line.)*

Left *While somewhat less glamorous, luxurious and innovative than her Gallic rival, Britain's* Queen Mary *was the most successful of all superliners. While other large ships such as the* Bremen, Rex *and the* Normandie *became war casualties, and the* Europa *passed into French hands to save a 'divided life', the beloved* Queen Mary *gave nothing but superb and distinguished service. She sailed for 31 years, carried well over two million passengers and made 1,000 crossings of the North Atlantic. She is said to have earned some £200 million ($600 million) in those three decades.*

Named by Her Majesty Queen Mary at the John Brown shipyards at Scotland's Clydebank, in September 1934, the 1,018 ft long Cunarder was soon afterward moved to a fitting-out berth (seen here), where the final stages of work resembled something similar to a giant jigsaw puzzle. Week after week, truckloads of fittings, furniture and all of the finer pieces of ocean liner creation arrived. There were 600 telephones and 700 clocks to be fitted onboard as well as glass in over 2,000 portholes and windows, and well over 5,000 chairs, sofas and tables. Components came from all over Britain. (Frank O. Braynard Collection.)

Right *The* Queen Mary *was delivered to Cunard in the spring of 1936, a year after the* Normandie's *first appearance and over six years since the first keel plates had been laid. During one long stretch, between December 1931 and April 1934, her construction was suspended, a victim of the financial chaos and depressed shipping conditions caused by the Depression, and she sat as a lonely, rusting shell of a ship, Fortunately, similar to the French Government's excited interest in their* Normandie, *London advanced considerable monies to Cunard to complete 'Britain's wonder ship'.*

Just prior to her maiden crossing to New York, in May 1936, the Queen Mary *took her turn in the specially built King George V Graving Dock at Southampton for inspection and final adjustment. One of her early predecessors, the* Majestic, *is berthed at the far left and is soon to go to the block (to become a boy's maritime training school and then be destroyed by fire). (Everett Viez Collection.)*

Left *While general design, luxury and passenger comfort were important aspects of superliner construction, the most important ingredient was record breaking speed. The coveted Blue Riband brought honour not only to the owners and the nation, but secured more passengers as well.*

In the bright glow of the floodlights at the King George V Graving Dock, the Queen Mary's *four huge propellors create an impressive sight. In her initial season on the Atlantic run, the propellors caused problems, not the least of which was considerable rolling and vibration to the ship. New propellors were soon cast and the fitted to the ship. Some of the disturbances were resolved, but for most of her seagoing career the highly popular* Queen Mary *was a rather notorious 'roller'. (Everett Viez Collection.)*

Right *Much like the* Normandie *and the other superships of the thirties, the* Queen Mary *was toured by tens of thousands of visitors. A magnificent 'ship of state', as these flagships were often called, every member of the British Empire contributed some element to her creation. The laurel wood used for the flooring in the first class lounge came, for example, from India. Other woods came from Canada, Australia, Ceylon, South Africa and New Zealand. The main lounge itself reached three decks in height and measured 96 ft in length. Among the dazzled visitors, souvenir hunters abounded. One enthusiastic woman was found, tools in hand, attempting to remove one of the paintings from a wall in a lounge. (Everett Viez Collection.)*

Above *The* Normandie *and* Queen Mary *were cross-channel rivals, among so many other ways, over record breaking and superlative statistics. The* Normandie *took the Blue Riband from the Italian* Rex *in the spring of 1935. The French liner's record stood at 29.98 kts against the Italian's 28.92. A year or so later, in August 1936, the* Queen Mary *grabbed the honours with a recorded 30.14 kts. The* Normandie *regained the penant, in March 1937, at 31.2 kts. The contest ended in August 1938, however, when the* Queen Mary *proved the faster, at 31.6 kts. Her record stood until the* United States *swept the seas forever, in July 1952, at over 36 kts. (Everett Viez Collection.)*

Left *When the* Normandie *was completed her gross tonnage was placed at 79,000. She was indeed the world's largest ship, having succeeded the 56,500-ton* Majestic *of 1922. Then, much to the discontent of her owners, the Cunard Company revealed that the* Queen Mary, *thought to be 75,000-tonner, would exceed 80,000 tons. The French could not be more displaced. Soon after the* Queen Mary *arrived with an overall figure of 80,774, the* Normandie *was hurriedly sent to drydock and had an otherwise unnecessary deckhouse built on one of her aft decks. Her tonnage increased to 82,779, then 83,423. For at least a few more years, the French would have, if not the world's fastest liner, at least the world's largest. (Everett Viez Collection.)*

Right *Just a few months prior to the* Queen Mary's *maiden crossing, in May 1936, Cunard formally announced that a long-awaited (and well planned) running mate would be built as well. Rumour was that she would be named* King George V. *While the* Queen Mary, *initially designed in the mid-twenties and therefore very much of a 'groundbreaker' and based on earlier ships such as the* Aquitania *of 1914, was an older, more conservative looking three-stacker, the new Cunarder would be far more contemporary. Cunard designers now had the advantage of factfinding, note-taking and even secret passages (often in disguise, no less) on such ships as the* Bremen, Rex *and* Normandie, *and even careful studies of improving the* Queen Mary. *The new liner would have, among other alterations, two instead of three stacks and far less cluttered upper decks. Sensibly, the building order went to the same Scot ship-builders, the John Brown Company at Clydebank, that had created the previous Cunard giants. This picture shows workmen streaming off the ship for their lunch hour. (Frank O. Braynard Collection.)*

Below *The new Cunarder was launched into the Clyde in September 1938, with an intended maiden crossing to New York scheduled for April 1940 (in fact, it never came to pass due to the outbreak of war.) The original choice of a name was abandoned and changed, quite thoughtfully, to honour the new, highly popular British Queen, Elizabeth, the wife of George VI. Accompanied by the 'little Princesses', Elizabeth and Margaret Rose, the Queen did the honours in the presence of nearly 500,000 spectators. With mighty roars, the rattling of chains and even small fires erupting along the slipway, the 1,031 ft long hull of the* Queen Elizabeth *was water-borne in just under two minutes. (Frank O. Braynard Collection.)*

Above *The Germans were rightly proud of their twin 'monsters', the 50,000-ton sisters* Bremen *(shown arriving off New York's Pier 86) and* Europa, *commissioned a year apart, in 1929 and 1930. The* Bremen *captured the Blue Riband from Cunard's venerable* Mauretania, *a prize she held for an unparalleled 22 years. A year later, the* Europa *took the record from her sister. Soon afterward, the* Bremen *improved still further and regained the penant. However, in 1933, it went to the* Rex *and then to the* Normandie *and finally to the* Queen Mary. *The Germans were less than pleased. They thought of building two larger, far faster Atlantic liners or, in a less ambitious mood, of installing new engines in the two earlier ships. Neither plan ever came to pass.* (Hapag-Lloyd.)

Left *A dramatic aerial view over the westbound* Europa, *steaming from Bremerhaven to New York via Cherbourg and Southampton. The twin German superships were less than great financial successes, both suffered from lingering anti-German feelings left from the First World War and then from the growing anti-Nazi sentiment of the mid thirties. However, like so many of the 'ships of state', it was most likely not expected. Instead, the return on their construction and high maintenance and operational costs was measured in international maritime prestige. The superships of the thirties, most especially, vied with one another for prized distinctions over their speed, size, decorative splendours, extraordinary service and envied cuisine.* (Frank O. Braynard Collection.)

In 1932, under Premier Mussolini's instigation, the Italians commissioned their first superliners, the 51,000-ton Rex and the 48,500-ton Conte di Savoia. They were the only 'ships of state' to sail out of Mediterranean waters, trading between Naples, Genoa, Villefranche, Gibraltar and New York. The more successful, the Rex, secured the Blue Riband for two years, beginning in August 1933.

Again, however, these ships were probably not expected to be huge profit-makers. Both carried far fewer passengers than anticipated, especially among the highly sought American tourist trade. The Italians worked tirelessly at promoting the 'sunny, southern route' to the Mediterranean, however. Among such features as outdoor swimming pools and aft decks lined with multi-coloured umbrellas, real sand was scattered about the upper, open air decks to create something of the 'Riviera afloat'.

In an exceptional occasion, depicted in the photograph right, the approaching Rex is seen from the topmost observation deck of the Conte di Savoia. Rarely did large liners, especially running-mates or sisterships, pass one another while underway. (Everett Viez Collection.)

While slightly smaller and less powerful, and therefore never a serious contender for the Blue Riband, the Conte di Savoia had her own distinction; the first 'roll-less' big liner. She was fitted with the then new gyro stabilizer system, a balancing device that predates the fin stabilizer units so commonly placed aboard contemporary ships. While certainly an immense advertising advantage, the devices aboard this Italian liner were, in fact, considerably less than successful. For example, they could not be used on westbound crossings because prevailing winds might seriously jeopardize the ship's balance. Consequently very often, the Conte di Savoia might be rolling about in the often treacherous North Atlantic like any ordinary passenger liner. (Richard K. Morse Collection.)

Top *Westbound on the Atlantic in the late thirties; the main lounge aboard the* Bremen. *(Hapag-Lloyd.)*

Above *A popular space aboard the Atlantic liners, the enclosed promenade. Bouillon at eleven and tea at four. The scene dates from 1938, aboard the* Normandie. *(Robert Russell Collection.)*

Right *The entire White Star Company was one of the saddest fatalities of the Great Depression. They never quite recovered from the tragic loss of their brand new* Titanic *in April 1912 and the firm's lustre was not quite the same by the twenties. Financial problems, among others, soon set in. White Star's transatlantic express liners, their 'Big Three', the* Majestic, Olympic *(seen here entering New York's Upper Bay in the early thirties) and the* Homeric, *began to falter in their arch rivalry with Cunard's giant trio, the* Berengaria, Aquitania *and* Mauretania. *The White Star liners were soon operating with reduced staffs and, according to some reports, were arriving in port scarred in rust. In 1934, under British Government insistence and supervision, the Company was merged with Cunard and became Cunard-White Star Limited, a title that lasted until 1950. (Everett Viez Collection.)*

SUPERSHIPS OF THE THIRTIES

Below *In the mid thirties, just as some of the most luxurious liners of all time left from the shipyards of Europe, the North Atlantic trade had actually slumped considerably, from over one million travellers in 1930 to less than half that number by 1935. Some ships went into 'mothballs', others directly to the scrapheap and all while several firms disappeared completely. The older big passenger liners, the 'floating palaces' from the pre-World War 1 era, survived just barely and then ran out of time. The clientele was gone, their prestige tarnished and the ships themselves often grew rather grubby and rust-streaked. Cunard's illustrious* Mauretania, *built in 1907 and which stood as the world's fastest (and therefore one of the most popular) liners until 1929, was among those that fell on hard times, in fact very hard times, by the early thirties. Repainted in white and as a last reprieve, she was sent on cheap cruises to 'nowhere'—'booze cruises' as the Americans called them—and sometimes further afield to Nassau, Havana and Kingston. In the autumn of 1934, she returned to Britain for the last time. Soon afterwards, the marble fittings and art treasures—among a near endless list of items—were tagged and placed on the auction block. Stripped and demoded, the old* Mauretania *set off on her last passage, to the scrappers at Rosyth in Scotland. (Cunard Line.)*

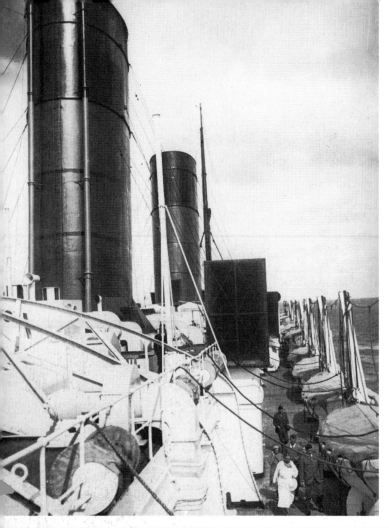

Left *Many of the larger, older transatlantic queens, such as Cunard's* Berengaria, *were detoured during the height of the Depression to inexpensive 'booze cruises'. Travelling beyond the legal limits of American Prohibition, the bars aboard these once highly popular transatlantic ships were opened to a thirsty public, members of which often paid as little as £2.15 ($10) a night for the privilege (and cabin). In addition, these voyages 'to nowhere' or to Halifax, Bermuda, Nassau or Havana, provided the ideal escapism, at least temporarily, from the bleak economic realities ashore.* (Everett Viez Collection.)

Below *While she once sped across the North Atlantic, on the luxury relay to Cherbourg and Southampton, the* Berengaria *spent greater time in the mid thirties on far more casual sailings, mostly bound for the tropics. Five days to Bermuda out of New York could cost £10 ($50). Her days were numbered, however. Originally commissioned in 1913, as the* Imperator, *the flagship of Imperial Germany and the world's largest ship of any kind, she was a victim of not only declining passenger loads and dwindling profits, but old age as well by the late thirties. Small fires, caused mostly by frayed and tired electrical wiring, began to cause considerable concern. At one point, American authorities even revoked her passenger permit. Shortly before Germany went to war once again, the* Berengaria *sailed for the breaker's yards.* (Everett Viez Collection.)

Above *Another former German, the* Vaterland *of 1914, was seized at Hoboken, in New York Harbor, during the First World War. Soon after, she raised the Stars and Stripes, and became the troop transport USS* Leviathan. *When hostilities ended, she was—after considerable deliberation and then renovation—restored as the flagship of the American Merchant Marine, the largest liner ever, in fact, to fly American colours. Unfortunately, however, her commercial career on the North Atlantic, as something of a lonely giant without a comparable running-mate, was far less than the expected success. By the early thirties, she began to spend more time out of service than in the Company schedules. Beginning in 1934, she was retired permanently, sitting out her final days (until January 1938) at her Hoboken berth—quiet, capped, partially stripped and layers of her paint falling into the waters of the Hudson. With little hope in sight, she was finally sold off to Scot shipbreakers at Rosyth. In this photograph, she is waved off on a bitter January afternoon. Thick blankets of blackest smoke, the first from her funnels in some years, hints of her final Atlantic crossing.* (Frank O. Braynard Collection.)

Right *Rattling, creaking, rolling from side to side and with her horns mysteriously triggered, the* Leviathan *crept across the Atlantic on her final passage. Manned by a small 'skeleton' staff, she would meet her onetime German fleet mate, the* Imperator, *which had become Cunard's* Berengaria, *at the Rosyth scrappers' yard. With the exception of the* Aquitania, *the great and grand 'floating palaces' from the pre-First World War era were finished. Once commonplace, the big four-stackers were almost extinct.* (Frank O. Braynard Collection.)

Left *Three of the* Aquitania's *four stacks as photographed by John Havers at the Southampton Docks in the late thirties. Tall, slender and gracefully canted, surrounded by ventilators, piping and deckhouses, and supported by webs of guidelines, such funnel arrangements had changed to the 'swept' upper-deck creations of ships such as the* Normandie, *where there wasn't an object of clutter in sight. (John Havers Collection.)*

Right *The towering masts of the largest ocean liners were slanted to match the rake of the funnels. A mass of rigging was attached to them, from the topmost fluttering flags to support wires to cargo booms that worked the express cargo in the forward holds. Within, in something similar to a vertical tunnel, a narrow ladder rose to that most solitary of posts; the crow's nest. Especially at the 'finger piers' of New York, these masts and, of course, the brightly coloured funnels seemed to rest above the upper pier sheds. Among the highest, this, the* Queen Mary's *forward mast rose over 200 ft from the waterline to the truck. (Fred Rodriquez.)*

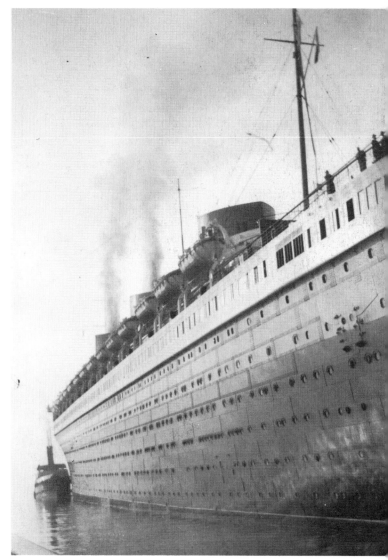

Left *To many observers, the liners were at their most impressive at dockside. At New York, the enormous bows would seem to rest against the very inner bulkheads of the ships and then extend, like vast skyscrapers placed on their sides, to the outer reaches of the berth. Little tugs, tiny barges and oil floats would come alongside these ships and produce the most dramatic contrast of dimensions. Overseas, such as the* Europa *at the Columbus Quay at Bremerhaven, the piersides had a slightly different dimension. Enormous limousines, taxis and porters' carts would crowd the docksides. In the adjacent sheds or outer dockland, great boat trains would arrive (from Berlin or Paris or London), delivering passengers that had travelled in classes of accommodation that often matched their shipboard quarters. Rail companies offered first, second and third class tickets. Passengers then boarded through long, often canvas-covered gangways. The voyage then began.* (Hapag-Lloyd.)

Right *At Southampton, among other ports, the largest liners—in a time-saving process—often anchored in the outer waters and loaded their passengers by tender. It was perhaps an equally dramatic approach to a ship; the huge form suddenly appearing out of a fog or the shimmering, reflective glow of night. In this view, John Havers has dramatically captured the extraordinary* Normandie *just after dawn, on 1 May 1937, off Ryde.* (John Havers Collection.)

Above *At least once a year, the liners took their turn in drydock. Resting upon specially placed 'blocks' and connected to shore by a series of gangways, ropes, cables, hoses and electric wires, the ships seemed to be momentarily at rest. Most of the ship's company would have been sent on leave while small crews of shipyard work teams painted, hammered, welded and scraped. Cranes, resembling tall, goose-necked birds, hovered over the upper decks, lifting off lifeboats (for refurbishing) or hoisting a workman in a 'basket' to repair a damaged funnel. At Southampton, especially for giant ships such as the Cunard's* Aquitania, *special all-day train excursions were organized from London to tour these drydocks and survey their huge contents. (Everett Viez Collection.)*

Left *Shipbuilding costs had risen sharply by the thirties. The Dutch, determined to build a brand new national flagship, were resourceful and most fortunate, however. Workers at the Rotterdam Drydock Company took voluntary wage cuts to secure the order for the country's biggest and finest liner yet, Holland-America's* Nieuw Amsterdam *of 1938. Even the Government had a role, offering low-interest loans to the ship's owners. When Queen Wilhelmina named the liner at the launching ceremonies, tens of thousands of guests and spectators were aptly proud and pleased. (Everett Viez Collection.)*

Above *Appearing to be the underneath portion of some huge sea creature, the twin starboard screws of the* Bremen, *in drydock at Bremerhaven, make for a most effective photograph. Notice the huge blocks of bolted wood on which the 50,000-tonner is mounted to the right, and the busy photographer with tripod on the left. (Hapag-Lloyd.)*

Right *Just as straight stems had given way to far more rakish designs, which greatly affected speed and bad weather performances, sterns had changed as well. The classically traditional style of the* Columbus *had disappeared in favour of cruiser styles, such as aboard the* Queen Mary, *or the counter design of the innovative* Normandie. *(Everett Viez Collection.)*

Canadian Pacific Steamships built one superliner in their long, diverse transportation history. Commissioned in 1931, the Empress of Britain, *at over 42,000 tons, was designed for an unusual service for such a large ship, transatlantic from Southampton to the St Lawrence River as far as Quebec City. By far, she was the biggest and fastest liner ever for the Canadian run. In winter, when the St Lawrence was ice-clogged, the 'great white Empress', as she was often called, was detoured to expensive luxury world cruising from New York, voyages of 130 days, 30,000 miles and visits to 35 ports. For these, full voyage fares began at £400 ($2,000). (Everett Viez Collection.)*

The old and new generations at Southampton in the late thirties; Cunard's new three-funnel Queen Mary *on the left and the veteran* Aquitania, *the last of the four-stackers, to the right. The older ship might have gone to the scrapheap, being scheduled for replacement by the brand new* Queen Elizabeth *in the spring of 1940, but the outbreak of the Second World War changed all plans. The* Queen Mary *left Southampton in August 1939, for what seemed to be a most ordinary, if exceptionally crowded passage (an anxious 2,139 passengers and evacuees were aboard), but then was ordered to remain in the safety of New York for the duration of the 'short political crisis'. Instead, she did not return to her transatlantic homeport (Liverpool was, in fact, her official homeport) for nearly six years. Similarly, the* Aquitania *joined the effort and gave heroic service in this, her second world conflict. (Everett Viez Collection.)*

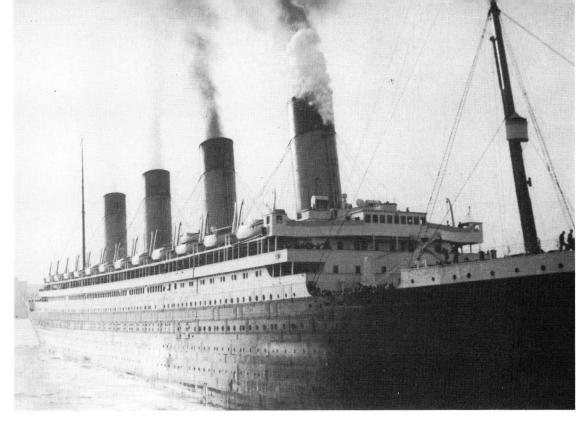

As the effects of the Depression reached more serious proportions, by the mid thirties, the Olympic *and all but one of the other four-stackers, those grand 'floating palaces' from before the First World War, steamed off to the scrapyards. The White Star liner is seen making one of her final New York departures, her steam siren on the first funnel being compared to a death rattle.* (Everett Viez Collection.)

By the autumn of 1939, almost all liner services had come to a screeching, most dramatic halt. The Queen Mary, Normandie, Ile de France *and brand new* Mauretania *were laid up at New York, awaiting the next events in a tense Europe. The* Queen Elizabeth, *still incomplete at Clydebank, was ordered—by direct command from Winston Churchill himself—to be finished and then to be sent to New York for safety. The* Bremen *and* Europa *were together at Bremerhaven, amidst rumours that the Nazis would convert them to aircraft carriers. The* Rex *and* Conte di Savoia *continued transatlantic service out of the Mediterranean, symbols of supposed Italian neutrality, until the spring of 1940. Finally, the* Empress of Britain *was hurriedly pressed into troop service, only to be sunk by October 1940, the first and largest of the supership casualties at sea.*

This poetic photograph of the Normandie *leaving Southampton Water at dusk, hints of the uncertainty, the change and the destruction in the years ahead.* (Everett Viez Collection.)

Chapter 2

Azure seas, louvered doors and exotic nights

The great liners, the recordbreakers, the 'ships of state' and the 'floating palaces', are perhaps best remembered at this distance in time. But, especially in the late thirties, in those years before the serious appearance of commercial aircraft, passenger ships—particularly smaller ones—provided links throughout the world. There were mailships, colonial liners, supply boats, immigrant ships and even peacetime troopers. A passenger ship map of the globe would show dozens upon dozens of lines, many of them overlapping, that criss-crossed the earth and stretched from Britain out to Australia or South Africa, from Japan to North America, from Holland to the East Indies, from Italy to Argentina and Brazil, from India to East Africa, and from New York to the very tip of the West Coast of South America. There is a nearly forgotten tale of a young Australian missionary nurse, who travelled first to New Zealand and then northward to Vancouver in one of the Union Line ships. After crossing North America by bus, she caught a Moore McCormack liner to Buenos Aires. Onward, she took one of the Dutch-flag Royal Interocean liners across to East Africa. From there, it was a British India ship to Bombay. After crossing India, she sailed from Calcutta to Singapore and then, aboard a little Blue Funnel ship, to Fremantle. The process took nearly two years.

Luxury, one-class cruising was perhaps the biggest new development of the thirties. Cruise travel had come to the masses, ironically in an age of Depression, mass unemployment and discontent. Assuredly, one of the reasons for the success of leisure voyaging, where the ports-of-call are less important and more of a diversion, is the very escapism that such trips provided.

While the first full cruise is reputed to have sailed in 1857, a Mediterranean jaunt aboard P&O's *Ceylon*, it remained the domain of the rich and super-rich until the start of the Depression. Even in the twenties, big ships such as the *Mauretania* and *Aquitania* went off to the Mediterranean from New York for six or eight weeks, but with as few as 200 millionaires aboard served by as many as 800 crewmen. Of course, cruising also developed as a profitable alternative to slump seasons in almost all trades, particularly on the bleak North Atlantic in deep winter. Sending a fully-booked liner to the warm waters of the Caribbean was far more successful than sailing half empty ships on the freezing, often stormy Atlantic. By the mid thirties almost all liners were cruising at least once a year.

Long-distance cruise voyages, supported by an older and richer following, had developed a strong popularity that began especially in the twenties and has continued to this day. Among the offerings from the large Raymond-Whitcomb Company for the winter of 1937 were:

'*Stella Polaris*, January 19th, from New York. The sixth annual Raymond-Whitcomb cruise to the South Seas, the East Indies and round South Africa to Europe. More complete than ever before, with visits to southern India, the Seychelles, Madagascar, South Africa, St Helena and West Africa. 110 days. Rates from New York to conclusion at Southampton, including shore excursions, $1135 up.'

'*Columbus*, February 6th, from New York. Completely around South America in 47 days. Through the Panama Canal, down the West Coast, through the Straits of Magellan and up the East Coast. With visits, in the *Columbus* or on shore excursions, to Lima, Valparaiso, Santiago,

Buenos Aires, Montevideo, Santos, Rio de Janeiro and other cities. Rates exclusive of shore excursions $545 up.'

'*Vulcania*, February 10th, from New York. A complete Mediterranean cruise in a Mediterranean ship. Six days in Egypt. Visits to famous Mediterranean cities, picturesque islands and towns. 43 days to Trieste. With return by Italian Line vessels sailing before June 26th. Rates, exclusive of shore excursions, $685 up.'

'*Champlain*, February 24th, from New York. The first cruise of its kind. With visits to Dominica, Martinique, Barbados, in the West Indies; Dakar in Senegal; Casablanca in French Morocco; the Canary Islands; Gibraltar, Algiers, Tunis, Paler o, Naples and Marseilles in the Mediterranean. 22 days to Marseilles. The cruise tickets will include return passage by French Line steamships sailing from Le Havre before July 15th. Rates, exclusive of shore excursions, $450 up.'

In the twenties much had been written about the large yachts of European royalty and aristocrats, and of the fabled American millionaire class. Consequently, Norway's Bergen Line built a specialized cruiseship, just over 5,200 tons, that was styled after such yachts. She was the highly popular *Stella Polaris*, commissioned in 1927, and designed particularly for those who appreciated long, leisurely and luxurious sailings, with all first class amenities, superb cuisine and precision service. For her passengers, the more extensive and more diverse the trip, the better.

Built at Gothenburg, Sweden, the new ship— 'the Star of the North'—was scheduled only for cruise service. Fitted with very high standard accommodations, she could never be anything but first class. Some 165 crew members all but hand-served an equal number of guests. There were four special de luxe suites, more than half the other cabins had private bathroom facilities and as many as one-third of her staterooms were for single occupancy only. Along with a series of beautifully appointed public rooms, a small open-air swimming pool was placed aft. Overall, the ship clearly resembled the yacht class. There was an ornate, scrolled clipper bow, twin masts, a single funnel and an all-white hull. From almost any angle, at almost any port, she looked handsome and serene. The *Stella Polaris* sailed regularly, apart from the war years, until 1969. She survives at present as a floating hotel, restaurant and yacht club off Mitohama Beach in Japan.

The Furness Bermuda Lines, a division of Britain's giant Furness Withy Group, is perhaps one of the most important early short-distance cruise companies. Beginning with small, second-hand steamers that traded between New York and Bermuda, their rather instant success by the mid twenties led to larger, more luxurious ships, namely the 19,000-ton *Bermuda* of 1927. A still larger running-mate, the *Monarch of Bermuda*, was added in 1931. Unfortunately, the *Bermuda* was destroyed in no less than three separate fires and had to be scrapped. She was replaced by a near-sister to the *Monarch of Bermuda*, which was aptly named the *Queen of Bermuda* and commissioned in 1933. These twin liners, handsomely designed, speedy and superbly decorated, were said to be the first cruise liners to match the standards of the famed transatlantic big ships. Among other amenities, they were two of the very first ships to have private bathroom facilities in all staterooms, regardless of price category. Operating in rotation on weekly sailings, on a six-day round trip, the pair became known as 'the millionaires' ships'.

The success of Furness and others in short-distance cruising, especially to such ports as Bermuda, Nassau and Havana, led to more extensive schedules by the late thirties. These voyages, mostly of a week's duration and agreeably priced, lured tens of thousands of 'new' sea travellers. In the thirties, particularly in the years just prior to the outbreak of war, cruising for the middle classes sprouted. The possible voyages were quite extensive, listed below in a one month schedule from New York in 1935.

Date	Ship	Itinerary
11 September	*Carabobo*	West Indies, 21 days
11 September	*Dixie*	New Orleans, 14 days
12 September	*Haiti*	Columbia and Panama, 18 days
12 September	*President Wilson*	Havana, 10 days
12 September	*Yucatan*	Havana and Mexico, 19 days
12 September	*Coamo*	West Indies, 11 days
12 September	*Peten*	Havana and Central America, 17 days
13 September	*Cottica*	South America, 17 days
14 September	*Santa Maria*	West Coast of South America, 39 days
14 September	*Santa Elena*	Intercoastal to California, 17 days
14 September	*Reliance*	Bermuda and Nassau, 7 days

Date	Ship	Itinerary
14 September	*Southern Cross*	Nassau, Miami and Havana, 10 days
14 September	*Oriente*	Havana, 7 days
14 September	*Atlantida*	Central America, 13 days
14 September	*Toloa*	Central America, 18 days
19 September	*Pastores*	West Indies, 18 days
19 September	*President Polk*	Havana and Panama, 17 days
19 September	*Nerissa*	West Indies, 25 days
19 September	*Orizaba*	Havana and Mexico, 19 days
19 September	*Borinquen*	Havana and Mexico, 12 days
19 September	*Veragua*	Central America, 17 days
21 September	*Lady Somers*	West Indies, 24 days
21 September	*Eastern Prince*	South America, 41 days
21 September	*Santa Barbara*	West Coast of South America, 39 days
21 September	*Rotterdam*	West Indies, 13 days
21 September	*Munargo*	Nassau, Miami and Havana, 7 days
21 September	*Oriente*	Havana, 7 days
21 September	*Pennsylvania*	Havana, 9 days
21 September	*Castilla*	Central America, 17 days
21 September	*Ulua*	Central America, 18 days
22 September	*Lady Nelson*	West Indies, 28 days
26 September	*Colombia*	South America, 18 days
26 September	*President Pierce*	Havana, 10 days
26 September	*Siboney*	Havana and Mexico, 19 days
26 September	*Coamo*	West Indies, 12 days
26 September	*Quirigua*	Central America, 17 days
28 September	*Santa Lucia*	West Coast of South America, 39 days
28 September	*Santa Paula*	Intercoastal to California, 17 days
28 September	*Pan American*	South America, 41 days
28 September	*Oriente*	Havana, 7 days
28 September	*Atlantida*	West Indies, 13 days
28 September	*Calamares*	Central America, 18 days
2 October	*Dixie*	New Orleans, 14 days
3 October	*Haiti*	West Indies, 13 days
3 October	*President Adams*	Intercoastal to California, 17 days

In these years port cities such as New York, Southampton, London, Hamburg, Lisbon, Capetown, Port Said, Bombay, Sydney and Hong Kong—among so many others—were rarely without at least one noted passenger ship in port. More often there might be as many as a dozen, scattered at various berths, being worked by barges and shoreside staffs, and which might remain in port for several days or even weeks. In today's cost-efficient cruiseship age, liners are rarely in port for more than twelve hours. At New York, in 1985, only two liners remained in port for overnight calls, the *Queen Elizabeth 2* and the *Rotterdam*, and both of these were in preparation for their annual three-month winter trips around the world. In the thirties, like all others, the transatlantic ships, both large and more moderately sized, ran with continuous frequency, in a comparable way to the aircraft departures at present day airports. At New York, departures for European ports during June 1937 were compiled by ocean liner enthusiast Richard K. Morse:

Date	Liner	Destination
1 June	*Europa*	Bremerhaven
1 June	*Pilsudski*	Gdynia
2 June	*Normandie*	Le Havre
2 June	*Aquitania*	Southampton
2 June	*Hansa*	Hamburg
2 June	*Washington*	Hamburg
4 June	*Statendam*	Rotterdam
4 June	*Laconia*	Liverpool
4 June	*California*	Glasgow
5 June	*Columbus*	Bremerhaven
5 June	*Vulcania*	Trieste
5 June	*Hamburg*	Hamburg
5 June	*Kungsholm*	Gothenburg
5 June	*Lancastria*	Liverpool
5 June	*Bergensfjord*	Oslo
5 June	*Reliance*	Hamburg
5 June	*Rotterdam*	Rotterdam
9 June	*Queen Mary*	Southampton
9 June	*President Roosevelt*	Hamburg
9 June	*Drottningholm*	Gothenburg
10 June	*Bremen*	Bremerhaven
10 June	*De Grasse*	Le Havre
11 June	*Cameronia*	Glasgow
11 June	*Samaria*	Liverpool
11 June	*St Louis*	Hamburg
11 June	*Veendam*	Rotterdam
12 June	*Conte di Savoia*	Naples
12 June	*Champlain*	Le Havre
12 June	*Georgic*	London
12 June	*Pennland*	Antwerp
16 June	*Normandie*	Le Havre
16 June	*Aquitania*	Southampton

Date	Liner	Destination
16 June	*Manhattan*	Hamburg
18 June	*Europa*	Bremerhaven
18 June	*Scythia*	Liverpool
18 June	*Transylvania*	Glasgow
19 June	*Berengaria*	Southampton
19 June	*Ile de France*	Le Havre
19 June	*Saturnia*	Trieste
19 June	*Deutschland*	Hamburg
23 June	*Queen Mary*	Southampton
23 June	*Pilsudski*	Gdynia
23 June	*President Harding*	Hamburg
25 June	*Carinthia*	Liverpool
25 June	*Volendam*	Rotterdam
26 June	*Rex*	Naples
26 June	*Britannic*	London
26 June	*Columbus*	Bremerhaven
26 June	*New York*	Hamburg
26 June	*Caledonia*	Glasgow
26 June	*Westernland*	Antwerp
26 June	*Stavangerfjord*	Oslo
29 June	*Bremen*	Bremerhaven
29 June	*Lafayette*	Le Havre
29 June	*Statendam*	Rotterdam
30 June	*Normandie*	Le Havre
30 June	*Aquitania*	Southampton
30 June	*Washington*	Hamburg
30 June	*Hamburg*	Hamburg
30 June	*Berlin*	Bremerhaven

[These sailings included additional ports of call.]

Passenger shipping in the thirties was also still in the great age of Empire, supplying the links between motherland and the far-off colonies. These 'imperial liner routes' seemed endless: from London out to Bombay or Hong Kong, Mombasa or even remote Fiji; from Marseilles to North Africa or farther afield to the Caribbean or Indo-China; from the Netherlands to the East Indies; from Belgium to the Congo; and from Italy to East Africa. Passenger ships, often medium-sized, but with adequate power to provide a scheduled link, especially for the mails, were guaranteed passengers, freight and therefore revenues without interruption. They belonged to the likes of the legendary P&O Lines, so well established that it was often referred to as 'the P&O', the British India Steam Navigation Company Limited, the Union-Castle Mail Line, the Orient Line, New Zealand Shipping Company and then the more exotically titled Messageries Maritimes, Chargeurs Réunis, Rotterdam Lloyd, Nederland Royal Mail Line, Compagnie Maritime Belge and Lloyd Triestino.

The ambiance and style of this era, the twilight in fact of the huge colonial fleets, is perhaps best exemplified in Charles Owen's *Independent Traveller*, which chronicles a homeward passage in P&O's noted *Viceroy of India*, sailing from Bombay to London via Aden, the Suez, Marseilles and Gibraltar:

'Experienced travellers to the East preferred her [the *Viceroy of India*] to even newer vessels entering the famous service connecting Britain, through Suez, with India and the Far East. The passenger list [415 first class and 258 second class] was headed by a majestic Commander-in-Chief, accompanied by mountains of baggage, a wife and an ADC. After lunch, I repaired to the lounge for coffee, choosing a pleasant table in the corner. Immediately, anxious stewards came whispering at me: if I did not mind, could I possibly sit elsewhere. . . this was His Excellency's favourite table. They were sure I would understand.

'Every first class passenger was pampered and had his ego stimulated to a gratifying degree. Everywhere servants waited to dance attendance on him—to bring him drinks, a quoit, a ping-pong ball, a paper hat; to point the way to the cinema, the gymnasium, the swimming pool. Repeatedly, through the leisurely course of every day and night, an orchestra—sweating politely under the punkah louvres—would take up its station in the palm-treed lounge, playing music to suit the moment. The grand climax in the small hours was a whirling series of old-fashioned waltzes, a gallop and finally, lights dimmed. . . that last exercise for flagging violins, "Good Night Sweetheart". Then the company would brace itself into immobility as the loyal strains of "God Save the King" floated out through the opened windows, across the moonlit decks and away into the tropical night.'

P&O was the best known and most historic of the colonial passenger shippers, British or otherwise, and had long established links not only with India, but with Suez, Australia and the Far East. Their passenger liners ranged from a quartet of 'express boats' on the London-Bombay route, that were evocatively named as the *Ranchi, Ranpura, Rawalpindi* and *Rajputana,* to austere little steamers such as the *Ballarat* and *Bendigo* that carried nothing more than over 2,500 souls in steerage on the long-haul migrant trade to Melbourne and Sydney. The larger *Viceroy of India* was the company's last traditional liner, completed in early 1929, and so typified the important Colonial flagship. Her decoration largely reflected the homeland, a design ingredient important to almost all imperial liners. In Peter Padfield's fine history *Beneath the Houseflag of the P&O*, he describes the interior of the *Viceroy of India*.

'Inside her deck houses are rooms which for furnishings and craftsmanship rival the best art in English houses of varying periods. Her first class smoking room was a magnificent echo of James I's old palace at Bromley-by-Bow with oak panelling, hammer beams in the dome above, a huge fireplace with carved overmantel, leaded windows with stained-glass escutcheons and wrought iron gates. The music room was 18th century style with lacquered pillars and pilasters, and a handmade carpet to match; the dining saloon decor was also 18th century with pillars in blue marble and seat coverings copied from old needlework preserved at South Kensington Museum. The reading and writing room was "Adam" with reproduction furniture and a mantlepiece with details copied from Harewood House, while the totally enclosed swimming bath was in the "Pompeian" style of classic pillars and panelled reliefs. Outside her promenade decks, with cunningly devised nooks, are long, wide and sheltered; the sports deck aft is a smoothly timbered floor of royal and inviting dimensions.'

Similarly, the glories of Holland were well incorporated into the decoration of the sisterships *Johan van Oldenbarnevelt* and *Marnix van St Aldegonde*, the new Dutch flagships of the East Indian trade, the fine art of a Belgian chateau aboard the *Léopoldville* on the Congo trade and reproductions of Parisian cafes aboard France's *Félix Roussel*, which worked the Saigon route. However, soon after the thirties began, a whole new generation of larger, finer and more comfortable ships began to appear on the colonial runs. If the *Viceroy of India* was the so-called last traditional liner in the P&O fleet, she was followed within two years, in 1931, by what appeared to be totally different ships, the sisters *Strathaird* and *Strathnaver*.

Known fondly as 'the Straths', followed by three near-sisters, the *Strathmore, Stratheden* and *Strathallan*, almost everything about them was new, fresh and innovative. Instead of the long familiar black hulls and black funnels, they were painted white overall and with bright yellow stacks. Their profiles, with three evenly slanted funnels (two of which were 'dummies' and added for effect) and two tall masts, were copied after some of the noted transatlantic ships. Like large yachts, sailing off to the tropics, through Suez from London and then onward to Aden, Bombay, Fremantle, Melbourne and

turnaround at Sydney, they appeared to be far more inviting. In fact, because of their light colouring, they were said to be at least ten degrees cooler onboard, an important consideration in reflection of the steamy passages through Suez, the Red Sea and Indian Ocean. Their passenger quarters were far more spacious, more contemporary and more comfortable. The Straths were the first P&O liners to have running water in all passenger cabins, for example. There were pools on deck, large open areas for games and canvas-covered hideaways. They were also designed especially to be convertible, spending the peak seasons on the Australian run and then cruising for the remainder. While migrants could travel out to Australia on a five-week voyage for as little as £8 ($40), other passengers went cruising to Scandinavia, the Canaries or the Mediterranean at £14 ($70) for an equal number of days.

These new P&O Straths produced a race of sorts during the thirties. Similar to the competitive spirit on the North Atlantic, other companies that sailed distant trades wanted newer, improved ships as well. The most notable addition of all appeared by 1935, Orient Line's *Orion*. While she was the first of the company's ships to use a light grey hull colouring (also for heat resistance in this non-air conditioned era), she was also the first major liner to use a single large mast. There was no aft mast and the required rigging was attached to her single stack. The exterior was, however, just a hint to the high modernity of this important ship. She brought the age of Art Deco, the era of transatlantic streamlining, to the Australian and later to other trades. The baronial splendours of earlier ships such as the *Viceroy of India* and such Orient liners as the *Orama* and *Orontes* were gone almost completely. Instead, she was bright, airy and totally spacious.

She was decorated by a New Zealander named Brian O'Rourke. He used large mirrors extensively which gave portions of the ship a fresh, almost open-air quality. Lacking fresh greenery or plants, floral patterns were deliberately worked into the carpets. A highly glossed veneer served as ceilings, which matched the richly polished tone of the hardwood floors. Throughout, the furniture was done in identical clusters. In the main lounge the overhead punkah fans were painted in white and matched the colour of the ceiling and columns. The very bright tone of this almost all white room was offset only by the 'marriage band' gold capitals. In the first class cafe, the tufted club chairs, seemingly brought directly from one of the new Atlantic Cunarders, were done in leatherette. There was even an Australian tavern, done with horse-shoe shaped chairs that were set around bolted tables. The flooring was done in plank-pegged strips while the long windows along the left end of the room could be opened on to the aft decks. The high praises for the *Orion* were soon repeated for a near-sister, the *Orcades* of 1937.

Similar new motifs and more inventive and stylish decorating were worked into other new ships as well. Shaw Savill's *Dominion Monarch*, finished in 1939 for the long-haul trade to Australia and New Zealand by way of South Africa, was a superb follow-up to the *Orion*. She was especially notable in that she carried only 500 passengers, all of them in first class accommodation, but in a ship over 26,000 tons. The Union-Castle Line, for their 'Cape Mail Express' run to South Africa, abandoned their earlier Tudor, Baroque and Adam stylings, and looked to the new 'moderne' as well. The new sisterships *Athlone Castle* and *Stirling Castle* of 1935–36 seemed well apart from the same company's *Carnarvon Castle*, built less than a decade before. The new ships would prompt even larger creations, namely the *Capetown Castle* of 1937, one of the largest motorliners ever built.

As the thirties drew to a close, there seemed to be a widespread renaissance in passenger ship design and decoration. Vastly superior ships, often copied from the likes of the *Orion, Stratheden* and even miniatures of the brand new *Queen Mary*, went down the ways. On the South American trade, to Rio, Montevideo and Buenos Aires, Britain added the *Andes* for the Royal Mail Lines

and France finished the *Pasteur* for the Compagnie Sud-Atlantique. P&O added a new ship, the *Canton*, for their Far Eastern trade and Union-Castle took delivery of their largest liners yet for the around Africa trade, the 17,000-ton *Durban Castle* and *Pretoria Castle*. The French proposed a striking new flagship for the Indo-Chinese trade, the *Maréchal Pétain*, and the Rotterdam Lloyd looked forward to a fast new flagship on the run to Batavia, a 23,000-tonner that would be completed after the war as the *Willem Ruys*. Another Dutch firm, the Nederland Line, added the *Oranje*, which so closely copied the earlier *Orion* that she too used only a single mast and funnel.

Unfortunately, it all ceased in that fateful late summer of 1939. John Havers recalled visiting the Southampton Docks, on 21 August. 'While visiting the *Orcades*, I noticed that the docks were full of guns and soldiers. A week or so later, on the 29th, I had my last visit as a civilian. Lamport & Holt's *Voltaire* was grey-painted and Royal Mail's *Atlantis* and Bibby's *Dorsetshire* were in hospital ship colours. This all seemed quite shocking as war had not yet come. The big Ocean Dock even seemed especially crowded; the *Queen Mary, Britannic, Lancashire* and the *Arandora Star* were at berth. I also noticed that those long-idle ships, the *Gloucester Castle* and *Edinburgh Castle*, had strangely disappeared. For those who watched the docks and closely followed ship movements to almost perfect accuracy, this all seemed most surprising and disruptive. A day later, on the 30th, the dock areas were closed to the public. My dock passes were discontinued!'

Left *Like most major transatlantic shippers, such as Cunard, White Star, Holland-America and the French lines, the Germans—namely the Hamburg American Line and the North German Lloyd—maintained 'auxiliary' fleets of passenger ships, smaller, often slower, less noteworthy vessels when compared to the giants of the preceding chapter. In this view, passing one another in mid-Atlantic, North German Lloyd's* Columbus *is about to overtake that same company's* Berlin. *Both are outbound from New York, destined for the Channel ports and then onward to Bremerhaven.*

The 32,000-ton Columbus, *commissioned in 1922 and often teamed with the large recordbreakers* Bremen *and* Europa *on the express service, was frequently sent on the Lloyd's more luxurious cruises; around South America or Africa, the Mediterranean and on the most fabled trips of all, three-month circumnavigations of the globe. The smaller, 15,000-ton* Berlin *was often sent on less opulent cruise sailings, one- and two-week runs from New York to Bermuda, Nassau and the West Indies as well as politically-inspired 'Strength through Joy' sailings with German workers and their families.* (Willie Tinnemeyer Collection.)

Right *As seen from the upper deck of the Lackawanna Railroad ferry* Elmira *as it plies its commuter run between Lower Manhattan and Hoboken, the steamer* Henry R. Mallory *of the Clyde-Mallory Lines heads for the Lower Bay and then the open Atlantic. Quite small, slow and with comfortable but limited accommodation, usually for first class only, she represented the busy, but final era of the American coastwise passenger liners. They sailed to Boston and Portland, to Norfolk, Charleston, Jacksonville and Miami, New Orleans and Galveston, and even on longer trips, via Havana and through the Panama Canal, to Los Angeles, San Francisco and Seattle. While still busy and running their diverse operations disappeared almost entirely by the end of World War 2. Improved and increased aircraft, rail and trucking competition dealt the decisive blows to this 'little fleet'.* (Everett Viez Collection.)

Left *The Hamburg-American Line, which owned the largest passenger liners afloat in the years just before the First World War, never regained their enthusiasm for very large, recordbreaking ships. The greatest efforts during the twenties were a team of 21,000-tonners known as the 'Famous Four', the* Albert Ballin *and the* Deutschland *of 1923-24 and their near-sisters, the* Hamburg *and* New York *of 1926-27.*

Like most of the transatlantic liners of the time, the Deutschland *(shown here during an early morning arrival at New York's Pier 84) carried three classes of passengers; first, second and third class.* (Everett Viez Collection.)

Right *Sailing for the Hamburg-registered Red Star Line, the 16,000-ton* Westernland *was specially refitted in 1935 to carry 550 tourist class passengers only. Running a transatlantic service between Antwerp and New York, it was a pioneer venture into low-fare, all-tourist class travel. Especially popular with budget tourists, immigrants, students and teachers, such sea-going operations might well be compared to the present age of airline 'no frills'.* (Everett Viez Collection.)

Above *Cruising became increasingly more popular during the thirties, prompted in no small way by the sinister Depression. Passengers sought escapism, and inexpensive sailings on otherwise well-served and well-fed ocean liners was the ideal solution. In this scene, Cunard-White Star's* Georgic *is departing from New York's Pier 54, with the Hudson River 'night boat'* Berkshire *in the background. Sailing on a late July afternoon in 1937, the* Georgic *is bound for a four-day 'Fourth of July' cruise to Halifax and return. Fares began at £6 ($29). Among near endless possibilities from dozens of shipping firms, Cunard-White Star schedules also included the* Scythia *for six days to Bermuda for £10 ($50); the* Samaria *for nine days to Havana and Kingston for £15 ($75); the* Britannic *for seventeen days to six Caribbean ports for £24 ($120); and the* Carinthia *for 47 days to the North Cape and Baltic Capitals for just over £80 ($400). (Everett Viez Collection.)*

Left *As part of the Panama Company's interests in the Canal Zone, three very modern combination passenger-cargo liners—the* Ancon, Cristobal *and* Panama—*were commissioned in 1939. They sailed on a weekly service, with passengers as well as considerable freight, between New York and Cristobal with a stop at Port-au-Prince in Haiti in each direction. As these ships delivered valuable cargo, supplies, foodstuffs and, a most important priority, the mails, to the Canal Zone, the stopovers in port were often lengthy, but well appreciated by passengers who used the ships for two-week roundtrip cruise-like voyages. (Victor Scrivens Collection.)*

Above *The Furness-Bermuda Line, a division of the huge Furness Withy shipping group, did much to develop the tourist virtues of the islands of Bermuda. Early second-hand passenger steamers were rather quickly replaced by specially designed, first class liners. The most famous and popular of these were the near-sisters* Monarch of Bermuda *of 1931 and the* Queen of Bermuda, *delivered two years later. They were among the first cruiseships to feature private bathroom facilities in every cabin and were especially noteworthy in being created with transatlantic style luxury but for the tropical trades.*

The Monarch of Bermuda *and* Queen of Bermuda *left New York each week, usually on six-day cruises to Bermuda, with minimum fares of $50 in the late thirties. Occasionally, however, there were extended voyages, such as the* Queen of Bermuda's *special visit to Nassau in the winter of 1938. The tender* Nassau *is alongside, taking excited tourists ashore for a day's touring, shopping or swimming. (Everett Viez Collection.)*

Right *Some steamer services appeared to be cruise voyages, but were, in fact, vital links of that mostly pre-aircraft age of the thirties. The Peninsular & Occidental Steamship Company's* Florida *ran a steady service between Miami, Key West and Havana. Very popular with many passengers, including a businessman's trade, many tourists took an outbound sailing for a vacation in the Cuban capital. After some time ashore in a hotel, they rejoined the ship for the return to the American mainland. From Miami, travellers often made train connections to points scattered throughout the United States. Many years later, in the late fifties, when the Havana service was curtailed due to political changes within Cuba, the* Florida's *owners sensibly detoured her to short-distance sailings between Miami and Nassau, another highly popular overnight run. (Everett Viez Collection.)*

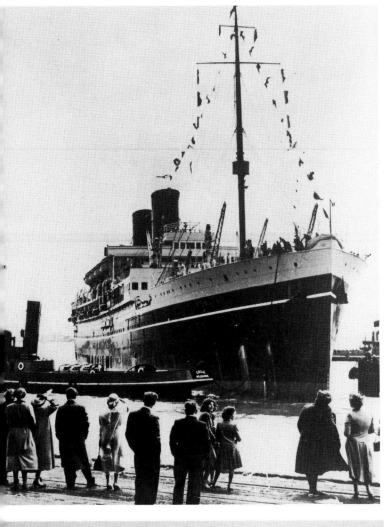

Far left *The thirties was, in so many ways, the final great age of Empire. Those vast social, economic and political links supported great shipping services. While freighters delivered the manufactured goods from the motherland and returned with the raw goods from colonial hinterlands, the passenger ships also had the steady flow of passengers; the high commissioners, the governors, the district superintendents and their accompanying entourages, the civil servants, the engineers, the traders and merchants, the troops and police, many of these often travelling with their families as well. Most ships on the colonial trades rarely sailed with empty berths.*

London's P&O Company, one of the most important and historic of all steamship companies and the most important ocean-going arm of the mighty British Empire, ran a very large fleet of passenger ships. Two of the largest and best known, the sisterships Maloja *and* Mooltan *(shown here) worked the Australian trade, from the London Docks outward to Gibraltar, Port Said, Aden, Bombay, Ceylon, Fremantle, Melbourne and Sydney. (P&O Group.)*

Left *In addition to the Australian trade, which was well supplemented by an enormous outward migrant trade, P&O liners sailed an express run to Bombay, and, for ships such as the 15,000-ton* Chitral, *on the Far East route. Shown berthed at Singapore, the* Chitral *and her sisterships, the* Cathay *and* Comorin, *plied a long-haul trade from London to Gibraltar, Marseilles, Port Said, Aden, Colombo, Penang, Singapore, Manila, Hong Kong and then to Kobe and Yokohama before reversing course for home. (P&O Group.)*

Left *Despite the almost guaranteed flow of passengers, there was considerable competition among the largest of the more distant passenger shippers. In particular, Britain's P&O Lines and their chief rival, the Orient Line, kept steady pace in building newer, larger, faster and better decorated liners. Most notable was perhaps the 'race' of the thirties. It began in 1931, when P&O introduced the first of their very popular 'Strath' liners, the 22,500-ton* Strathnaver *(seen here, outbound and taking a plunge by the bow). She and her sistership, the* Strathaird, *not only reduced the passage time between London and Sydney via Suez from six to five weeks, but were the first Company liners to feature running water in all passenger cabins, both in first and tourist class. They were also the first to be painted overall in white, which not only gave the ships a more tropic guise, but reduced the temperatures in the frequently steamy passenger quarters by as much as ten degrees. So impressed and delighted were they with this pair, that P&O soon ordered three near-sisters, the* Strathmore *of 1935 and then the twin* Stratheden *and* Strathallan *of 1937. (John Havers Collection.)*

Above *The Orient Line responded to P&O's new 'Strath' liners with a very distinctive pair of large sisterships, the 23,500-ton* Orion *and* Orcades *of 1935-37. In overall design, they were the first major liners to dispense with the traditional two masts and instead used only one, forward mast. All rigging was attached to the single funnel. Furthermore, as something of a compromise between the customary black hulls of the earlier ships on the Australian trade and then the innovation of all-white hulls on the new P&O liners, the Orient Line decided upon a dove-grey hull colouring. It too had helped to cool the non air-conditioned interior. Internally, the* Orion *introduced the very contemporary Art Deco stylings to the Australian run. Rounded columns, high gloss floors and an extensive use of stainless trims and swirl-design carpets had been previously seen only on the major Atlantic liners, such as the* Normandie. *Thereafter, decoration on many long-distance, overseas liners copied the* Orion. *(Pat Laing Havers Collection.)*

Left *The traditional styling aboard the colonial liners, such as P&O's* Viceroy of India, *built in 1929 and used on the London-Bombay express run, reflected the baronial splendours of Britain. Company directors and decorators felt that passengers, especially in first class, would appreciate the vivid reminders of home, no matter how remote in styling. Gracefully-turning ceiling fans provided the only mechanical ventilation in what might be seen as an otherwise 'untropical' setting. On the three-week (or longer) passages out to India, there were long days in shaded deck-chairs with a good book, ten-course luncheons and dinners, afternoon teas, some after-dinner games or bingo in the lounge, or brandies and cigars in the smoking room. (P&O Group.)*

Right *Passage from Sydney, aboard the* Stratheden, *1938. (P&O Group.)*

Left *Cabin accommodation on the colonial runs had improved considerably from the age of Kipling and first governors of the Raj. A first class single cabin, aboard the* Orion *of 1935, included hot and cold running water, forced-air ventilation, ample cupboard space, a private shower and toilet and a full window that looked out onto the sea below. Among other onboard amenities, passengers had the use of a good number of well furnished public rooms, a fine restaurant, shops, a bank and excursions office, a bar pub, open-air swimming pools, large decks for games and deck-chairs, and even a squash court. (P&O Group.)*

Right *The dog-racing team, aboard the* Viceroy of India, *in the mid thirties. (P&O Group.)*

Disembarking at Port Suez, from P&O's Mongolia, *1936.* (P&O Group.)

For the important Dutch colonial run to the East Indies, the Nederland Line of Amsterdam built the largest ships yet, the 19,000-ton sisterships Johan van Oldenbarnevelt *and* Marnix van St Aldegonde *of 1930. Each carried four classes of passengers. Along with the government administrators, the civil-servants and their families, the rubber, spice and tea merchants used these ships for their frequent travels to the far-off colonies. When sighted from shore, these ships often represented a most joyous sight. They were often delivering family members, relief personnel and medical and missionary forces as well as cargo holds of mail, furnishings, food, appliances and other highly-prized goods from the motherland. In the scene below, the* Johan van Oldenbarnevelt *is making a special call at Belawan Deli on Sumatra. Two small inter-island steamers, from the Dutch KPM Company, are berthed to the right.* (Nedlloyd Group.)

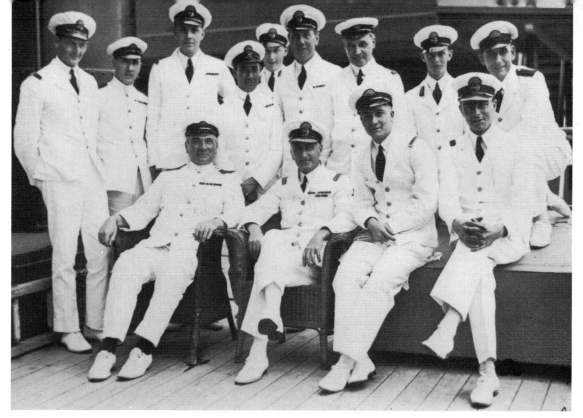

The Captain and officers of P&O's Maloja. (P&O Group.)

The French had colonial passenger services to North and West Africa, to South-east Asia, the South Pacific and to the Caribbean and South America. The Compagnie Generale Transatlantique, also known as the French Line, handled the Caribbean trade, to the islands of Guadeloupe and Martinique. Among the larger ships on that route was the 18,400-ton De Grasse, *built in 1920-24 and fitted to carry 536 passengers in cabin class and 410 in third class. Later sunk by the retreating Nazis at Bordeaux during the final days of the Second World War, she was salvaged, then refitted and—because of severe war casualties—singlehandedly reopened the French Line's express service between Le Havre and New York. She returned to the Caribbean briefly in the early fifties, before being sold off to Canadian Pacific to become their* Empress of Australia *and then to Italy's Grimaldi-Siosa Lines for service as their* Venezuela. *In 1962, when over forty years old, she was stranded off Cannes and, being uneconomic to repair, was sold to nearby Italian scrappers at La Spezia. (Everett Viez Collection.)*

Another of Britain's most famous passenger firms was the London-based British India Steam Navigation Company Limited. Maintaining a large fleet of mostly passenger-cargo ships, which often carried as many as four classes, a long-distance service was run from London, via the Mediterranean and Suez, to ports along the East African coast. A second fleet was based at Bombay for sailings to East Africa and the Persian Gulf, and from Calcutta to South-east Asia and the Far East. The 9,100-ton Modasa *worked the London-East African trade and is seen above at Marseilles. Much like the P&O and Orient liners, the call at Marseilles was a practical alternative to the five or so days in- or out-bound from Britain. Not only did passengers often prefer to avoid the notorious Bay of Biscay, but the express trains from Marseilles to Paris and then to London were faster than the sailing time.* (Marius Bar.)

The British passenger ship fleet was the largest and most widespread of all until the early sixties. Its decline corresponded with the gradual demise of the country's vast overseas colonial holdings. While the Union-Castle Line ran the prestigious 'Cape Mail Express' to South Africa, as well as a 'Round Africa' run, that completely circumnavigated the continent, passenger service to West Africa was worked by the ships of the Liverpool-based Elder Dempster Lines. Their combination ships, carrying mostly first class passengers, travelled to such ports as Freetown, Lagos and Takoradi. The company's 9,300-ton Apapa, *built at Belfast in 1927, was one of the largest ships of this service.* (Fred Hawks.)

Similar to their European colonial neighbours, the Portuguese maintained a fleet of passenger ships for the links to African Angola and Mozambique. Outbound from Lisbon in 1939, the Colonial *is given a special farewell escort as a governor general is aboard. (Luis Miguel Correia.)*

Another British shipper, the Bibby Line, handled the trade out to Burma. In 1921, they reached into another trade; peacetime trooping under charter to the British Government. Among the ships used for this service was the 9,600-ton Dorsetshire, *which had been refitted especially to carry over 1,500 troops, officers and dependent families. As the troop charters, sailing to outposts in East Africa, the Middle East and Far East, were seasonal in nature, ships such as the* Dorsetshire *spent several months each year in 'lay-up', at anchor in the River Dart. Used during the Second World War as a hospital ship, she saw considerable post-war service as well; as an Australian migrant ship, returning Dutch nationals from troubled Indonesia, a workers' accommodation station at Aden and even a final stint of peacetime trooping, during the Mau Mau troubles in East Africa in the early fifties. (J. K. Byass.)*

Chapter 3

Painted in grey, the war years

On 1 September 1939, as Hitler's forces slammed into neighbouring Poland, the lights of Europe abruptly went out. War had started. Shipping services on the North Atlantic, especially for passenger ships, came to a screeching halt. All that remained were the still-neutral American liners, namely the sisterships *Washington* and *Manhattan*, which turned immediately to 'evacuation service', first from France and then later from Italy and finally Portugal. The Italians continued as well, a supposed symbol of the Mussolini government's neutrality, with their two largest ships, the superliners *Rex* and *Conte di Savoia*. Both continued on the New York run, although with far less eastbound passengers, until the following spring. Soon thereafter the ships were withdrawn as the Italians joined the Axis powers.

In the early fall of 1939, New York—among other ports—was a quiet haven to a mighty fleet of suddenly idle liners. The *Normandie* and *Ile de France* sat across from the already grey-painted *Queen Mary*. On the opposite shore of the Hudson, in Hoboken, the Dutch *Nieuw Amsterdam* was caught in a similar limbo. Government ministers advised shippers such as Cunard and the Holland-America Line not to risk such important ships at sea. Their schedules were cancelled, their crews reduced and their future purposes uncertain. These ships, vehicles of such gaiety and luxury in better times, now sat quietly, almost in loneliness, creaking as they shifted with the changing tide, but otherwise looked after only by rotating teams of diligent maintenance and security crews. As the *Mauretania* arrived, having been considered far too great a possible target at the Liverpool docks where she had been kept, the *Ile de France*, under the care of a special team of tugs, was moved to an even more remote berth on distant Staten Island, in the outer reaches of New York Harbor. She seemed a most unusual and mighty sight while berthed at a cargo terminal. The Dutch, seemingly more adventurous and not yet officially at war, sent the *Nieuw Amsterdam* on a specially created programme of West Indies cruises, taking mostly Americans who were still able to ignore the sinister clouds on the horizon. She continued to sail to the tropics until May 1940, when she was urgently recalled just after the Nazi invasion of her homeland.

The *Bremen*, the powerful flagship of the German merchant navy, was nearly retained at New York. Arriving in port on 29 August, she was due to sail the following day, mostly with Americans, on her regular run to Cherbourg, Southampton and Bremerhaven. The commercial sailing was promptly cancelled as American authorities insisted upon inspecting the ship, deck by deck and to every last storage locker, for possible munitions or other objectionable goods. Once cleared, she was given permission to sail, in fact to make a bold dart for the safety of home waters. On the 30th, a reporter for *The New York Times* wrote:

'As twilight fell, the liner *Bremen*, her long reaches of deck empty, save for the occasional white-jacketed steward or blue-clad officer, slipped away from her West 46th Street dock with a band playing German airs. Unlike many other occasions of the past, when the two immense buff-colored stacks were illuminated by piercing floodlights and the cabins filled with passengers eagerly looking forward to whatever lay before them in European resorts, the great liner slipped away almost furtively down the river, with every light extinguished except the running lights required for navigation.'

The mood, both aboard the ships and in most ports, had indeed changed. John Havers recalled visiting the *Bremen* just weeks before, at Southampton, on 30 July:

'I went out by tender to the *Bremen*. To my complete surprise, she was anchored just opposite Portsmouth, the big British naval base. She was beyond the boom defence nets, which stretched across from Portsmouth to the Isle of Wight. However, for the first time, I was quite happy to leave a ship. There were lots of Nazi salutes onboard and "We Will March Against Britain" songs. It was a very unpleasant atmosphere. I knew then that war was inevitable [although still a month or so off]. The visit really brought home the threatening headlines. As the tender left the *Bremen*, all the crewmen lined the upper decks and gave the Nazi salute. Their message was simple and direct: "We'll have you later!" To add mystery to the occasion, a strange speedboat encircled the *Bremen*.'

Like so many of his countrymen, John Havers promptly joined the Services in early September, just as the war erupted. 'Because of my ship knowledge, I was immediately commissioned as a sub-lieutenant and taught coding and decoding. I revisited the docks for the first time "in uniform" on September 20th and saw the troopers *Athlone Castle*, *Alcantara*, *Pennland*, *Glenearn* and two 'neutrals'—the American *President Harding* and the Dutch *Colombia*. A week later, on the 28th, I attended the group sailing of the *Athlone Castle*, *Alcantara*, *Empress of Australia* and *Franconia*. In October, there were 98 ships in Southampton, among them the *Aquitania*, *Capetown Castle*, *Orcades*, *President Harding*, *Somersetshire*, seventeen cross-Channel steamers and lots of requisitioned yachts. A very rare sight was the little *Acadia* of America's Eastern Steamship Lines [an intercoastal passenger ship that had never crossed the North Atlantic]. By the end of 1939, we heard lots of rumours that the brand new *Queen Elizabeth* was due, but this was in fact "disinformation".'

George VI and Queen Elizabeth were to have visited the nearly complete *Queen Elizabeth*, Cunard's second supership and the biggest liner afloat, in late September. The visit was obviously cancelled. All work ceased on the ship as attention shifted to more urgent military and warship contracts. Several months later, permission was received from London to fit out the *Elizabeth*, but only with necessary equipment and all of it in

preparation for a highly secret plan to get her away from the British Isles.

Winston Churchill, as First Lord of the Admiralty, suggested that the new Queen be sent to North America, preferably to New York, in the safe company of her intended running-mate, the *Queen Mary*. The commercial maiden voyage had been set for April 1940 but was all but forgotten—the innovation of a twin-ship transatlantic luxury shuttle would have to wait, for as long as seven years, until the summer of 1947. A deliberately plotted rumour had been set that the liner would, soon after leaving the John Brown yards on the Clyde, go to Southampton for further drydocking and fitting out. This seemed a logical sequence, in fact one used by the *Queen Mary* four years earlier. Instead, in high drama and the tightest secrecy, once the *Queen Elizabeth* left the mouth of the Clyde she fled, with little warship escort, at top speed and in radio silence, for the north of Ireland and then into the open Atlantic. Even the river pilot stayed with the ship. Her 400 crew members were even unsure of her destination. Rumour was that it might be Halifax. On the date of her intended appearance in the Channel and arrival at Southampton, the Luftwaffe were waiting overhead. It was a brilliant, daring escape for the second of the greatest Cunarders.

The *Elizabeth* reached New York in early March, dressed in wartime grey, still incomplete, without her passenger fittings and deprived of the customary gala reception of tugs, fireboats and pleasure craft. She took her place on the north side of Pier 90, at the foot of West 50th Street, and just across the shed from her three-funnel companion, the *Mary*. The *Normandie* was alongside adjacent Pier 88. Awesome, majestic but silent, the three biggest liners ever built remained together for a fortnight. Provisioned, repainted and with boilers fired, the *Queen Mary* left New York with hardly a notice, bound on the longest journey of her career to date, southward to the Caribbean, then along the South American coast and across the South Atlantic to Capetown, and finally out to Sydney. Taken in hand by local shipyard crews, her transformation into one of the world's two largest and most important troopships began. Much of her luxurious peacetime fittings were removed and sent into storage. Cunard steward Len Houghton recollected: 'I came out to Sydney in the 35,000-ton *Mauretania*, the first big Atlantic liner to arrive, and we caused great excitement. But when the *Queen Mary* reached the Australian port, we were completely pre-empted.'

The *Mary* was assigned to Indian Ocean duty, which included a return voyage to Britain as well, but which mostly meant to reinforce the Middle East and North Africa. Outwards she would carry Australian and New Zealand forces; homewards, with considerably less loads, there would be evacuees, the wounded and prisoners. She joined one of the war's greatest troopship convoys in that spring of 1940. While the *Mary* was the largest unit, her fleetmates were quite impressive: Cunard's *Aquitania*, the last four-stacker; Canadian Pacific's transatlantic flagship, the 42,000-ton *Empress of Britain*, as well as their transpacific flagship, the *Empress of Japan*; and the Royal Mail Lines' brand new flagship, the *Andes*. Months later, on similar voyages in such distant waters were the *Queen Elizabeth*, which sailed in sight of the *Mary* on several occasions, the *Ile de France* and the *Nieuw Amsterdam*.

The Queens, like almost all troopships, travelled on zigzag courses, kept highly secret and mostly with radio silence. Of course the two giant Cunarders would have been most desirable targets, while quite often the Japanese were no more than a day off their positions. It was with great fortune that they survived unharmed. John Havers was posted out to the Suez area and recalled his first sighting of the new *Elizabeth*:

'I shipped out in August 1940, aboard P&O's *Strathnaver*, which was one of the last big ships to leave Southampton. Luftwaffe planes were overhead and photographed us, but we somehow managed to sail onward in safety. We stopped at Capetown en route to Colombo on Ceylon. I then transferred to British India's *Ekma*, a 5,000-tonner, built in 1911, that was bound for the Red Sea to Port Suez. We were part of an enormous convoy of troopers, which included P&O's *Ranchi*, the French *Félix Roussel* and dozens of "BI" [British India] boats.

'There would be thirty or more troopers in Suez Bay at any time. One certainly had to know his ships as they were all in grey and with painted-out names. It was only by silhouette that identification might be possible. The troops were transferred from these ships by Nile ferries, all of which were piloted by turbaned Sudanese captains. These men were proudest to serve the biggest ships. At first, the *Aquitania* seemed most important to them with her four big funnels.

'Later, I was sent down to safe anchorage T, in the Gulf of Suez, which was opposite Mount Sinai, to buy outright for the Director of Sea Transport the hospital ship *Atlantis*. This necessitated taking an inventory of everything aboard that belonged to Royal Mail Lines, her previous owners. It was the summer of 1941. After several days there, the *Atlantis* was ordered up to Suez and I went with her up the Gulf and back into the range of the Nazi torpedo bombers operating from Crete. This took place overnight and the *Atlantis* was fully lit with red crosses illuminated, etc. The Nazi planes found us and flew overhead, but respected our status. When we arrived at Suez in the morning, the *Queen Elizabeth* was just dropping anchor and it was my first sight of her ever. It transpired that she had been just in front of us while the enemy aircraft had their eyes on us. They had actually flown right over the *Elizabeth*, but had not seen her due to her perfect blackout. This poses the question: Was the *Atlantis* a stooge to attract the pilots' attention or was it a coincidence? The *Queen Elizabeth* did not normally stay in Suez overnight as all 'the monsters' were disembarked quickly using every craft possible, the main ones being trans-Nile ferries. The most valuable ships would then steam down to Tor or safe anchorage T for the night and then return to Suez to embark during the day.'

By mid 1942, the Queens were further refitted to carry as many as 15,000 troops, over seven times their intended peacetime passenger capacities. With the exception of the dining halls and a few lounges, every possible space was transformed into sleeping quarters, mostly in the style of collapsible canvas cots. In an agreement made between Prime Minister Churchill and President Roosevelt, the giant Cunarders were reassigned to the North Atlantic, to work a steady relay, almost as if on a peacetime timetable, but on a far more northerly course, to Gourock in Scotland instead of Southampton. They would again be blacked out, and would zigzag, silenced, using their top speeds. Able to outpace any form of military escort and far too valuable to risk in sluggish moving convoys, their course patterns changed, mostly dependent on U-boat sightings, from as far south as the Azores to northern waters off Iceland. Very few were privy to the exact movements of the Queens.

Mr E. W. Neighbour of Shortlands in Kent recounted a voyage in the troopship *Queen Mary*, in December 1942, on her final detour off the North Atlantic. Carrying 10,669 troops, including 160 women, she left Gourock for the Suez via Freetown, Capetown and Aden.

'Coming up from Blackpool, the weather had improved and we were able to see a considerable stretch of the River Clyde, and to my personal surprise, I could see in the distance down river the huge silhouettes of the liners *Queen Mary* and *Queen Elizabeth* lying at anchor. After some delay, inevitable in service life, we got away from the quay and began speculating upon which ship we were destined to travel in. It was soon evident that it was to be the three-funneller, and as we came round the stern of her, we could plainly see the name *Queen Mary* under the grey warpaint.

'We drew alongside, and after more delay, only a couple of hours this time, I found myself aboard the *Queen Mary*, having entered by a loading door only a few feet above the waterline. I was then handed a mess card and a berth ticket, the latter marked "A-129 Starboard Mattress", which rather dispelled my vision of a luxury cruise. I was waved toward a passageway and almost immediately became lost. The ship was absolutely alive with troops, all dragging kit-bags, rifles, etc, and trying not to look as though they had never seen the inside of a ship before. Considerably later, I stood in the doorway of A-129, wondering how I was to get any further. In peacetime, this was a first class double cabin, with all the luxury that went with it, but in 1942, it presented a different spectacle. All unnnecessary and some necessary fittings had been removed, including the door, and three three-tier bunks put in. These nine bunks were already occupied when I arrived, which explained the meaning of the word 'mattress' on my berthing ticket. Two more of us had to kip down on the deck between the bunks. With a small mountain of kit, rifles, lifejackets, etc., we had a right to complain of overcrowding, but somehow we eventually sorted ourselves out. It was alright if you kept your elbows in!

'Having dumped my kit, I wandered on deck to look for some of the lads from my own unit. The question of food was now of paramount importance as the box of rations issued at Blackpool and our water bottles were nearly empty. Therefore, I hopefully joined one of the three or four queues which wound the corridors and staircases. But it was soon evident that the messing arrangements were quite inadequate to deal with the hungry multitude of troops. So, deciding to subsist until morning, I finally got between two blankets about midnight and, in spite of the discomfort, was soon dead asleep.

'On waking the next morning, I was immediately aware that the *Queen Mary* was no longer as solid as a rock beneath my feet, but was alive with power and movement, and a never ending creak of partitions and bulkheads as the ship rolled. We were on our way.

'Hurrying to the boat deck that first morning at sea, I was just in time to see land disappearing in the mist astern, presumably the western isles of Scotland. There was a rough looking sea and it was bitterly cold. Many eyes scanned the horizon for signs of our escort, but we were quite alone and apart from a Flying Fortress, which kept us company for a short while later that morning, we sighted no vessel of any kind for the next eight days.

'The essential business of feeding nearly 11,000 hungry troops must have presented quite a problem to those whose responsibility it was. Eventually, order came out of the chaos, reflecting considerable credit on the catering staff. Messing was arranged in four sittings, which meant that the meals all but overlapped. The queue began on A Deck and wound its way along passages, down staircases, to the main dining hall, now stripped of its peacetime splendour and fitted with long tables and trestle seats. This was a slow business, in consequence we spent many hours squatting on our lifejackets awaiting the rattle of the irons and mess tins which signalled even the slightest forward movement of the queue. The food could not be described as tasty, but I remember the white bread, a real luxury in 1942, and the American marmalade in large bowls parked at the end of each table.

'On the second day, the *Queen Mary* was rolling heavily in typical winter Atlantic weather: cold, raining and with an ugly sea. The zigzag course which we were steering worsened the motion. [The course of the ship from Gourock to the Cape was in the form of the letter Z, with a stroke added at the top.] A plague of seasickness swept through the ship, the never to be forgotten stench being indescribable. Happily, I wasn't badly affected although I felt very green for a few hours. Gone were the long queues for meals so that those of us who felt well enough to face food were able to call the dining hall our own. For two days, the *Queen Mary* plunged through seas which few of us had witnessed before, and many were the bruises and not a few broken bones suffered. After one terrific lurch, I found myself on top of a heap of bodies at the bottom of the main staircase aft after having but a moment before been a couple of steps from the top.

'It was about the third day out that we turned south, killing the rumour that we were bound for Canada or the USA. The weather steadily improved as we got into warmer latitudes, and familiar faces began to reappear in the meal queues, although I knew of some who were ill for nearly a week. By the sixth day, we were sailing in brilliant sunshine and comparatively calm seas, the time when most tried on the uniform with which we were to become so familiar, known as the K.D. The ventilating system in the *Queen Mary* was not built to cope with the tropics and it became unbearably hot below decks. At night, the upper decks became packed with men sleeping nose to tail. There was a strict blackout in force, the consequence being severe, even for smoking. In spite of overcrowding and discomfort, the sleeping on deck under the tropical stars is to me one of the outstanding memories of the voyage.

'On the morning of the eighth day, "land in sight"—those magic words—created a stir in the ship. I was soon on deck to catch my first glimpse of the West African coast. We were approaching the entrance to Freetown harbour. Soon after, as we moved slowly through a flat calm, the great ship appeared to touch bottom, making the water thick with mud. We seemed almost to stop and then suddenly we felt the throb of the engines at full power taking the ship clear of danger. As we approached the harbour, a Swordfish aircraft made its appearance and flew round the *Queen Mary* at boat deck level. It was coastal command's effort to protect us from subs. We anchored some way from shore among a group of AMCs [Armed Merchant Cruisers] and immediately became aware of the terrific heat of the tropics. The coming of darkness brought some relief, but we hadn't counted on a plague of insects which invaded the ship. We all donned our slacks, rolled down our sleeves and there was a great smearing-on of anti-mosquito cream, a concoction which we learned to despise. In our ignorance, we imagined that each insect carried a deadly fever and a hopeless war was raged against them and much sleep was lost. The following afternoon, we were thankful to feel the sea breeze once more as we moved slowly past the boom defence and out to sea. I only remember Freetown as a collection of red roofs amongst dense green foliage shimmering in the heat. By sunset, we had lost sight of land and were steaming at full speed for Capetown.

'For the next four days as we zigzagged our way south and well toward the South American continent in perfect cruising weather, many of us crossed the Equator for the first time. None of the usual ceremonies were held. Perhaps Father Neptune was deterred by the noise of our 6 in anti-submarine gun, which carried out a practice shoot on this day, firing at a red float dropped over the stern. We were often startled by one or other of many ack-ack guns carrying out practice shoots without warning, although they did help to boost morale.

'Soon after leaving Freetown, drinking water was strictly rationed, a water-bottleful only which had to be drawn before 8 am causing long queues in the early hours. In the tropical heat, we were unable to satisfy our thirsts, and many a man must have dreamt of ice cool drinks. Gradually, the weather got cooler, till on the eighth morning out of Freetown, we awoke to find land on the port beam, low sandy hills with blue mountains away in the distance. Coming to the rail, I could see right ahead to the famous Table Mountain, with the Capetown harbour beneath. We still had some way to go to our anchorage, but already a tanker was coming alongside and soon we were surrounded by all sorts of craft engaged in the operation of revictualling. Many men had visions of a run ashore, but it was not to be and we had to be content with feasting our eyes on one of the most beautiful natural harbours in the world; what a pity we could not use our cameras. For two days we anchored in Table Bay, but then, without fuss or warning, we were off on the next lap, destination unknown.

'Soon after leaving Table Bay, the *Queen Mary* ran into the bad weather usually associated with the Cape route: high seas and continuous rain combined to make life uncomfortable aboard. Having sailed so many miles alone, it was a surprise to see a destroyer zigzagging ahead of us, the seas sweeping her from stem to stern, at times only the topmasts and funnel being visible. She did not stick it for long however, and after an exchange of signals on the Aldis lamp, returned to the shelter of Capetown. For the next three days, a considerable number of men took little or no interest in life aboard as, for the second time during the voyage, a plague of seasickness swept through the ship, leaving the dining rooms to those fortunate few with strong stomachs. Gale force winds whipped the seas into a frenzy, and men were thrown about the sloping decks like nine-pins, with boat drill a daily adventure. I pondered on how the sailing ships of days gone by used to make this passage and still survive.

'Having got round the 'bottom' of Africa, the weather steadily improved until we were once more sailing in wonderful tropical conditions and here again it was hard to imagine that a bitter war was raging or that an enemy sub may at any time disturb our complacency. No doubt, those who were responsible for the well-being of the ship had different feelings.

'The Equator was crossed for the second time, and as we steamed north the question was "India or the Middle East?" Canada, America and Australia were now out of the reckoning. Nine days out of Capetown, we thought we had the answer as land was sighted in the shape of sand covered hills shimmering in the heat, the approaches to Aden. My memories of Aden are rather faded now, but there sticks in my mind the picture of a destroyer steaming slowly round the *Queen Mary* the whole two days we were anchored there. Doubtless the Navy were glad when we left. Most of us wondered how far we could endure this heat, but it is amazing how the body becomes acclimatized in a few months.

'It was almost dark as the *Queen Mary* began to move slowly away from her anchorage in Aden, the start of what was to prove the last lap of our voyage, the longest that most of us would ever make. It was late the same night, about 11.30 pm, when the first real incident of the voyage occurred. It was a glorious tropical night, calm sea under a canopy of stars blazing in a pitch black sky. Some thousands of us were sleeping on the top decks to escape from the heat in the cabins below (it was particularly bad in the depths of D, E and F decks) when, without warning, the great ship turned, heeling over at an alarming angle and causing considerable confusion among the sleeping forms. I had staked a pitch on A Deck, in the large space forward of the main staircase, known in peacetime as Piccadilly. I awoke to find myself lying half on top of the adjacent "bod". There was noticeably more vibration in the deck as extra speed was put on. However, anti-climax followed as things soon returned to normal, and although it was a subject of conversation next day, we did not discover an authentic answer. Some had it that a Jap sub was the cause and others spoke about unidentified aircraft flying over.

'The following morning found us steaming up the Red Sea at 30 kt for the first time on a straight course, with land clearly visible on the port beam, just a low line of sand hills. I remember we passed a lighthouse built at the tip of a spit of sand, a lighthouse reputed to be the loneliest in the world. Signs of our journey's end were now evident, my own contribution being some four hours in the oven heat of the forward hold shifting baggage to the lifts, followed by a long search for my own kit bag among the hundreds of "deep sea" kit bags piled everywhere on the promenade deck. The cabin was simply a mass of kit-bags, webbing, rifles and all the paraphernalia we used to lug about those days, and with all these landing preparations in progress the atmosphere and routine of the ship which we had known for nearly a month seemed to vanish. We began to get orders appertaining to our departure from the ship, and we wondered vaguely what sort of a place Egypt would turn out to be.

'Speed was reduced that evening, and with it the efficiency of the ventilating system, the knowledge that we were lucky to arrive in the coolest time of the year was of little comfort. Leaning on the rail next morning, I had my first view of desert country at close quarters, as we proceeded slowly towards Port Tewfik, the sand looking almost white in the glare of the sun.

'Anchoring a mile or so from the port, the *Queen Mary* was soon surrounded by an assorted collection of native craft, mostly the barge type in which we were destined to make the final lap to Egyptian soil, or more correctly sand. Breakfast was the last meal organized aboard, but if I remember right, some kind of rations were issued to sustain us until next we might have the opportunity of getting a proper meal. My recollections of the following four or five hours are of mainly hanging about awaiting the word to disembark, but eventually I found myself, with the other chaps of the unit, facing a gaping hole in the side of the ship from the dizzy height of A Deck. Beyond, suspended by a derrick, was what I believe is known as a bosun's ladder, zigzagging down the side of the liner to the tenders alongside. I shall always remember negotiating that ladder. With a seemingly insecure rope as a handhold, loaded or rather overloaded with kit, and the whole structure swaying sickeningly, there was not a man among us who was not glad to reach the tender safely. One man just in front of me managed to drop his Sten Gun, but by some miracle it fell into the water between the tender and the ship's side. Being of an imaginative turn of mind, I became apprehensive of receiving a sharp blow on the head. As we chugged towards the shore, I looked back at the great liner, a grand and majestic sight amid the sandhills and blue sky to which our eyes were to grow so used.

'For some days to come at the notorious camp of Kasfareet, men could be seen walking with a "rolling gait".'

On the North Atlantic troop shuttle, the two big Queens were known as the 'grey ghosts'. They were the phantom ships—sailing under cloaks of high secrecy. The sight of one of these grey-painted giants left indelible impressions. In wartime Frank J. Watson Jr of North Andover, Massachusetts, was a crewman aboard the US

Navy non-rigid patrol airship K-80. On 13 October 1943, they received orders to take off before dawn from the Lakehurst Naval Air Station in New Jersey and to fly out into the Atlantic for about 250 miles to intercept the inbound *Queen Elizabeth* and then escort her to outer New York Harbor in the vicinity of the Ambrose Lightship.

'My job in the crew was that of "airship rigger", which in flight meant that I acted as relief rudderman or forward and aft lookout or either of the three on demand, so that I had excellent visibility at all times. We carried radar, magnetic detection devices, four depth bombs and some early versions of sono-buoys for tracking submerged subs.

'In the morning, we picked up the *Queen Elizabeth* on radar at about 60 miles and approached her to identify ourselves, which seemed hardly necessary as we had US NAVY in 10 ft high letters on both sides of the bag. Flying at only about 450 ft and slowing down from 60 to 40 kt, we had a marvellous view of the ship. She was running alone at high speed. As we got nearer, a very few people could be seen on deck. However, in a few moments, hundreds of people came out—all waving while we were hanging out windows and waving back. We had the feeling that our blimp was the first sign they had seen indicating they must be close to New York. Walking wounded could be seen, judging from the crutches and casts, plus some nurses in uniform and many men in military uniforms. All seemed delighted to see us.

'We ranged out ahead of the *Queen*, keeping a sharp lookout for submarines. None were seen. It was later learned that the main thrust of the German U-boat campaign had been moved south to the Caribbean and Gulf of Mexico area. At dusk, we returned to the base, having been 15 hours, 36 minutes in the air. A very interesting flight and a change from escorting plodding 10 kt convoys.'

While the Cunard Queens established heroic records, the very best of any two liners used in war service, many other passenger ships, particularly the superliners of the thirties, were far less fortunate. By the war's end, the only pre-war superships left in operable condition were the highly successful *Queen Mary* and Germany's *Europa*, which had spent most of the war years in idleness and neglect at her Bremerhaven pier. Cunard's *Aquitania*, the last of the four-stackers, was also afloat, but far too elderly to restore for further luxury service.

Canadian Pacific's *Empress of Britain*, while homeward bound from Capetown and Freetown to the Clyde, was attacked and set afire by Nazi bombers when only 70 miles north-west of Ireland. One of the bombs made a direct hit on the ship's first class main lounge. All but 49 of her 600 passengers and crew were saved. Burnt out and blistered badly, she was placed under tow, but two days later, on 28 October 1940, she was hit with two torpedoes from an enemy submarine. Rather quickly, she slipped under and became the largest Allied merchant ship to be lost in the hostilities.

Several months later, on 16 March 1941, the laid-up German *Bremen* was set afire by a discontented young crew member. A quiet Sunday afternoon, the blaze spread quickly on the otherwise unguarded ship. She was completely gutted and then nearly sunk against her pier by tons of water from the firefighters. Later, she had to be scrapped and her remains sent to the munitions factories.

The twin Italian superliners died a year apart. The *Conte di Savoia*, which had been laid-up in an anchorage near Venice, was hit by Allied bombers on 11 September 1943. She burned out completely and then sank in shallow waters. Her blackened corpse, minus upperdecks, funnels and masts, sat grotesquely in dishonour and disgrace. While thought was given to salvage, mostly as a restored emigrant ship, she was later found to be unworthy and went to local breakers in 1950. A year after the bombing of *Conte di Savoia* on 8 September, the *Rex* was hit by 123 rockets from RAF bombers while anchored in the Gulf of Muggia, south of Trieste. She burned from end to end, and then rolled over and sank. Scrapping began in 1947.

One of the most pathetic losses of the war took place in the safety of New York Harbor, however. The magnificent *Normandie* had been laid-up since the late summer of 1939 and was not seized by American authorities until after the attack on Pearl Harbor, in December 1941. Officially, she was renamed USS *Lafayette* and was to be converted to a huge trooper, similar to the Cunard Queens, while at dockside at the former French Line passenger terminal. As the liner was stripped and most of her luxuriant fittings and art treasures sent ashore, and as workmen followed a rather frantic pace, carelessness became apparent. On the cold afternoon of 9 February, the sparks of an acetylene torch ignited some kapok lifejackets and the blaze spread rapidly. The former *Normandie* was soon abandoned and in flames from end to end. Midtown Manhattan was covered in a thick orange-brown smoke.

Frank Braynard recalled that infamous afternoon.

'I was a student at Columbia University at the time, getting my Master's Degree or perhaps it was when I was trying for my PhD. I decided to cut classes and see a movie downtown. As I was walking to the subway, I heard fire engines racing all over the city and fire sirens going off— everywhere it seemed. Little did I realize that the *Normandie* was burning. I got to 42nd Street and saw my silly movie. When I came out of the theatre, the sky was all brown, light brown. Smoke hung everywhere and I knew something dreadful was taking place. In no time I was over at West Street [along the Hudson River shore] and trying to see what was happening. I could not get even close but hung around and hung around. It was terrible and later I interviewed the *Normandie*'s famed designer Vladimir Yourkevitch, who told me how he had tried to get Navy permission to board the ship and open her sea cocks. Had this been done, the great liner, the greatest of all time, would not have tipped over. Admiral Adolphus Andrews, Commander of the Third Naval District, brushed Yourkevitch's suggestion aside with a brisk: "This is the Navy's job!"'

In the pre-dawn hours of the following morning, the 10th, the *Normandie*—heavily overloaded with tons of water from fireboats, tugs and shore equipment—capsized at her berth. She was lost forever. While the fire had been damaging, the firefighting methods were indeed the killing blow. The fire damages might well have been repaired, but on her side, stuck in the Hudson River mud and stretched between two 1,100 ft piers, she presented the most difficult salvage job in history. The US Navy was mortified. Richard Morse recalled the sight of the capsized liner, in an article entitled 'Requiem for a Goddess':

'It was a blustery Lincoln's Birthday, the 12th of February. Our country had been at war for about two months, and the news from all parts of the world was uniformly bad: Europe was under the Nazi heel, Singapore was tottering under Japanese attack and ships were being sunk off our East and Gulf coasts.

'I stood, together with a close friend, at the corner of West 49th Street and 12th Avenue, viewing one of the most tragic sights ever: the burned-out, capsized wreck of the grandest passenger liner ever built, the *Normandie*. She had been done to death by catastrophic carelessness and monumental stupidity.

'Here was the absolute high point of marine architecture, lying there like some fat, sodden fishwife, totally helpless and useless. I began to recall earlier times when I had visited the *Normandie* and marvelled at her sumptuous interiors, a sort of Radio City Music Hall gone to sea. I remembered that 300 ft long first class dining room, the fantastic decorations of all her public rooms, enchantments in lacquer and glass—a true temple of Art Deco. This liner had had a winter garden with live birds, tapestries that might well put Bayeux to shame, artifacts in hammered bronze—I could go on forever. As I recalled these better, happier days, I began to cry. Here was an entire era destroyed in one stroke of carelessness.

'My friend and I both bade farewell to the *Normandie*. She was ultimately raised from the Hudson River mud and then towed to a Brooklyn backwater, but she was good only for scrapping. To this day, I still mourn her loss; such magnificence had never been equalled. Farewell, thou goddess. Thy likes we'll never see again.'

After a tedious, highly planned salvage that cost $5 million, the $80 million *Normandie* was eventually sold to scrappers at Port Newark, just west of New York Harbor, for a scant $161,000.

As the war in Europe and then in the Pacific came to a close in that spring and summer of 1945, the passenger ship business had changed considerably. Over a third of all liners afloat in 1939 had been destroyed. How many of them, such as the brilliant *Normandie* or the *Bremen* or the *Rex*, would have continued and for how long? Would the *Normandie* have lived to the customary retirement age of thirty and then been enshrined as a great floating museum? Certainly, she would have been the ideal candidate.

Soon after Hitler's forces slammed into Poland in that fateful late summer of 1939, many liners sat out the uncertain months ahead at the safety of their berths, preferably at New York. Upon orders flashed by their respective Governments, both the Queen Mary and Normandie were kept at their Manhattan berths. Holland's Nieuw Amsterdam was at first laid-up as well and then detoured to Caribbean cruising. The sister-ships Washington and Manhattan, flying their still neutral American colours, were rerouted for evacuation service out of the still peaceful Mediterranean.

While far newer and more important ships such as the Queen Mary could not be immediately risked at sea and therefore remained at New York for over six months, the veteran Aquitania was among the first large liners to leave the New York docks, repainted in grey military disguise, for diverse, top secret war service. While she was to have been replaced by still incomplete Queen Elizabeth in the spring of 1940 and then scrapped, the 'Ship Beautiful', as the Aquitania was often dubbed, went to war in another international conflict. By 1945, she had steamed an additional 500,000 miles to ports around the world and carried a further 300,000 passengers. She survived, in fact, until 1950, the very last of the glorious four-stackers, after a post-war stint of transatlantic austerity service between Southampton and Halifax. (Frank O. Braynard Collection.)

Other Cunarders sat out the 'political limbo' of the autumn of 1939 at their Manhattan berths. With the majority of their crews being sent home on smaller, less important ships, those once busy Atlantic liners were looked after by small maintenance crews and under the watchful eye of the company's New York office. By the late winter of 1940, however, with firm orders in hand, many of these liners were despatched, under highly secret orders and with veiled voyage plans, to destinations throughout the world for military duty. The brand new Mauretania, commissioned in June 1939 and shown resting at Chelsea Pier 54, between the Scythia on the left and the Samaria on the right, returned to sea in the following March, bound for Sydney via Panama, San Francisco and Honolulu. (Cunard Line.)

The Ile de France *was one of the most beautiful and popular liners on the North Atlantic. Commissioned in 1927, she introduced early Art Deco as decorative motif for passenger ships. An immediate success that marked the end for earlier stylings such as Baroque, Tudor, Palladian and French Louis XIV, the sleek, glossy, very streamlined decor of the* Ile de France *was soon termed 'ocean liner style'. Ranking among the finest of all passenger ships, she was, of course, a forerunner to the most magnificent of all, the* Normandie, *which appeared eight years later.*

The Ile de France *was caught at New York in September 1939, and there remained on order from her Paris-based owners. For over eight months she sat at a distant pier, off Lower New York Bay, looked after by a bare staff of one hundred. Afterwards, she too was plunged into war. In sombre greys and blacks, she dashed to the Mediterranean and then out to the Far East, where she was claimed by the British following the fall of France. For the duration, the* Ile de France *sailed under dual flags, those of Britain and Free France, and was managed first by P&O and then Cunard-White Star.* (French Line.)

America did not officially enter the war until December 1941 and American passenger ships continued trans-atlantic sailings until well into the spring of 1940. To avoid attack by ever-lurking Nazi U-boats and aircraft, they wore large, very visible 'neutrality markings' along their sides and upon their upper decks. The Washington, *shown berthed alongside another United States Lines' passenger ship, the* President Roosevelt, *at New York Piers 60 and 61, was rerouted off the Northern Europe service to the Channel and Hamburg and sent instead first to Bordeaux and then Genoa for evacuation service. The* Washington, *built to carry some 1,200 peacetime passengers, was urgently carrying three times that number on often tense westbound trips to New York. Passengers without actual cabin accommodation gratefully settled for specially arranged cots in the public rooms.* (Everett Viez Collection.)

Left *As the North Atlantic became less and less safe, American liners were rerouted to safer waters. Among others, the liner* Manhattan *was sent on intercoastal cruises, from New York through Panama to California. On one trip, in January 1941, she ran aground on a sandbar some 150 yd off the shore at Palm Beach, Florida. Her 200 passengers were promptly sent ashore by launch, but the 705 ft long liner remained stranded for 22 days. When finally freed and with her twin propellers bent, she had to be towed homeward to New York at an extraordinary cost of over £50,000 ($2 million). The* Manhattan *never sailed again as a commercial passenger ship. During the repairs, it was decided to outfit her as the troop transport* Wakefield. *She was never restored after wartime service and remained in lay-up until she was scrapped in 1965. (Everett Viez Collection.)*

Below *The brand new flagship of the American merchant marine, the 33,500-ton* America, *was launched on 31 August 1939, the day before the Nazis peacebreaking attack on Poland. The liner was intended for transatlantic service, beginning in the summer of 1940. In fact, all plans were soon shelved. When completed, the* America *was kept in Caribbean and then intercoastal cruise service. Shown passing through the Panama Canal's Culebra Cut for the first time, in February 1941, she was later given over to the US Navy and became the trooper USS* West Point. *Over the next five years, until early 1946, she carried thousands of passengers in grey disguise; soldiers, officers, the wounded, prisoners, evacuee and even exchange personnel. It was said that the* West Point *was the best known American wartime troopship and that she boasted of more onboard card games than the biggest casino ashore and served more Coca-Cola than any restaurant or soda fountain. (Everett Viez Collection.)*

Right *One of the most secretive, heroic and successful of the wartime passages of the great liners was the urgent dash of Cunard's brand new* Queen Elizabeth *from her birthplace on the Clyde to the safety of New York. When war erupted in that September, the world's largest liner was still incomplete, being scheduled for her maiden voyage in April 1940. Immediately, all but the most essential work was suspended and, under special orders from Winston Churchill himself, the ship sent across to less perilous waters. While the dock space at the John Brown Shipyards was needed for more pressing warship projects, the* Queen Elizabeth *was also in danger, in fact a sitting target, to the Nazi Luftwaffe. Under a huge disguise, with a rumoured destination of Southampton, where the Luftwaffe were, in fact, waiting, the 83,673-tonner slipped out of Clyde in late February and then sped—travelling north of Ireland, completely blacked-out and in radio silence—for an 'unknown' North American destination. Even her 400 crewmembers were unsure of the liner's final routeing. (Frank O. Braynard Collection.)*

Below *When the* Queen Elizabeth *safely reached New York, she was already painted over in grey and, on special request from Cunard, was not accorded the customary fireboat welcome. She slipped into New York Harbor late on a wintery afternoon, 'a dark-veiled empress incognito' as one newspaper called her, and did not even respond to the bellowing salutes from other ships in port. A small reception committee from Cunard and the British Admiralty welcomed her as she slipped into her berth on the north side of Pier 90. She took her place with the two other largest ships then afloat, the* Queen Elizabeth, *which can be seen just behind the stacks of the two Moran tugs, and the* Normandie, *seen on the far right. Awaiting further orders, they sat in silent majesty, creating an awesome trio that was known to New York dockers as 'the monsters'. (Frank O. Braynard Collection.)*

Left *The* Queen Mary *and* Queen Elizabeth, *respectively the world's fastest and world's largest liners at the time, were the most important troopships of all time. The Cunard Company, their designers, builders or initial crew could not have envisaged their invaluable roles. Stripped of their peacetime fittings, they were eventually fitted out to carry as many as 15,000 troops per voyage (this against their intended commercial capacities of approximately 2,000 each). Going to war, in March and November of 1940 respectively, they first served far from home waters, on a relay from Australia to the Middle East and later to Suez. In 1942, they returned to the North Atlantic for their best work, steady rotation on the 'GI shuttle', between New York and Gourock in Scotland (the Channel ports were far too dangerous during the war yars). (Victor Scrivens Collection.)*

Below *Every conceivable space aboard the Queens was used by the troops. With nearly eight times their intended capacity onboard, they carried the greatest numbers of all time. The* Queen Mary *(shown here) has the absolute record, made in July 1943, when she sailed eastbound with a total of 16,683 onboard. (Frank O. Braynard Collection.)*

Above *The comforts of the pre-war days were virtually non-existent on the wartime Queens. The first class suites, for example, were reworked to accommodate as many as two dozen officers; first class double-berth rooms might sleep as many as eighteen. The public rooms were converted as well, to large dormitories for 300-400 servicemen. There was no privacy among those often worried solider-passengers. Meals were served in as many eight twenty-minute sessions each for breakfast and dinner; there was no lunch. The elegant tables of fine crystal, starched linen and ten-course menus had given way, as seen here in the* Queen Mary's *first class restaurant, to hardwood tables, long benches, and metal bowls, plates and utensils. Kidney stew was a common wartime offering. (Robert Lenzer Collection.)*

Right *Throughout the war, until the late spring of 1945, the Queens worked the North Atlantic on blacked-out, radio-silent, highly-secret courses. To and from Gourock, the patterns were changed—from as far north as Iceland and south to the Azores—based mostly on enemy U-boat intelligence. Too fast for warship escorts except when close to either shore, the twin giants used their maximum speeds very often. With warning, they could out-pace any U-boat or torpedo. These liners, which transported a total of nearly two million wartime personnel and which, according to Churchill, helped to lessen the war in Europe by at least a year, were aptly termed the 'grey ghosts'.*

This view, from the crow's nest of the Queen Mary, *shows two of her specially-mounted guns. In fact, both Queens carried rather slight armament when considering their value, purpose and cargoes. (Robert Lenzer Collection.)*

Liners of all ranks and sizes were called to duty during the Second World War. They were, however, often difficult to identify. Painted over in greys or special camouflages, their names and marks of identity were obscured. In some cases earlier names were changed. They often travelled far from intended waters, and appeared in ports quite suddenly.

Matson Line's Mariposa, built in 1931 for the South Pacific run from California and with space for some 750 passengers, was refitted as a troopship in late 1941 with space for over 5,000 soldiers. Thereafter she wandered the globe—to such ports as Freetown, Capetown, Karachi, Bombay, Rio de Janeiro, Marseilles, Liverpool and Reykjavik. Although she was returned to her owners undamaged conditions had changed considerably and she was not restored for American service. Instead, after several years awaiting her fate, she was sold off in the early fifties, to become the Panamanian-registered Homeric of the Home Lines. (Victor Scrivens Collection.)

During the war many liners were altered, both for special duties and as a form of disguise. Furness-Bermuda's Queen of Bermuda, a three-stacker during commercial times as seen here, was reduced to twin funnels during her military service as an armed merchant cruiser and then as a troop transport. After the hostilities, her third stack was returned. However, in 1961-62, during a major modernization refit, all three funnels were replaced by one, wide device. Consequently, the Queen of Bermuda is the only liner to have sailed as a one-, two- and three-stacker. (Alex Duncan.)

The importance and value of passenger ships, especially as troop carriers, had increased considerably during the War. The efforts to save such ships were very often extreme. Consequently, when, in September 1942, the troopship Wakefield—*the former* Manhattan *of the United States Lines*—burned at sea during a westbound crossing from the Clyde with 950 evacuees onboard, all considerations were used in the attempt to save the ship. A small closet fire on B Deck had spread rapidly so that the entire ship was soon engulfed and then abandoned completely. Ten days later, the still smoldering near wreck was taken in tow and beached in a cove near Halifax. While the last remaining fires burned out and even with very sensitive stability, inspection teams from the US Navy thought salvage to be worthwhile. Recommissioned in the spring of 1944, at great cost and effort, she lost an entire upper deck in the process and became a full time military transport. This photograph shows her after completion of repairs. (Victor Scrivens Collection.)

Converted liners often sailed in large, slow-moving convoys. As many as a dozen diverse passenger ships might be included in each while one of the largest convoys of all, numbering over 150 merchant ships, departed from New York in 1943. In this scene, from 1941, three former luxury liners are delivering troops. Holland's Johan van Oldenbarnevelt is to the left; P&O's Canton *is the centre position; and another P&O vessel, the* Viceroy of India, *is to the right and closest in view.* (Richard K. Morse Collection.)

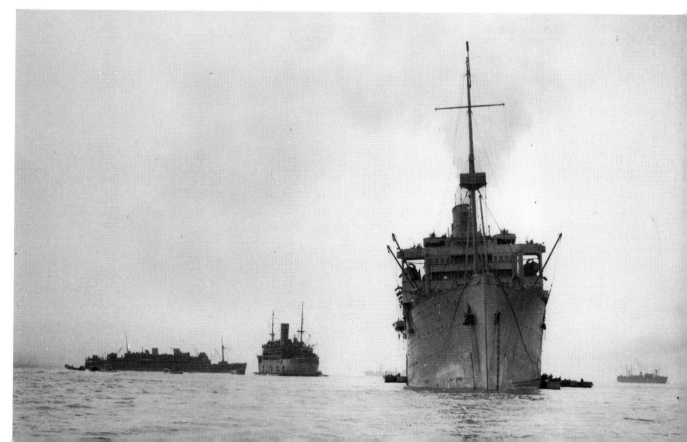

Especially in the early war years, some ships remained in familiar waters while in troop service. In this scene, at Sydney in the winter of 1940, P&O's Strathnaver *is about to depart with the first Australian troops bound for the defence of the Middle East and North Africa. In the background, also soon to be loaded with military passengers, is the Orient Line's* Orcades. *After the war the* Strathnaver *would reappear with a modernized single-stack look; the* Orcades *would be struck from the lists, having been torpedoed off the Cape of Good Hope in October 1942. (John Havers Collection.)*

Over 200 passenger ships were lost during the Second World War, from bombings, torpedoes, fire and even sabotage. In this scene, the Apapa *of Britain's Elder Dempster Lines has been hit by Nazi bombers and is burning from end to end. The date is 15 November 1940. (Richard K. Morse Collection.)*

The Apapa, *sinking by the stern, takes the final plunge.* (Richard K. Morse Collection.)

Most of the large Italian liners, like the German ships, were kept in home waters during the war years. Regrettably, most of the Italians were later sunk, either by the retreating Germans or by Allied bombings. Two of the larger ships, the motorliners Saturnia *and* Vulcania, *built in the late twenties for the run between Trieste, Venice and New York, made successful bids for Allied waters. They were hurriedly converted for more important trooping duties. The* Saturnia *was given even further assignment, becoming the* Frances Y. Slanger, *honouring the first American nurse to die in the War, the largest army hospital ship afloat. She was fitted out to carry 1,300 litter and 388 ambulatory patients. She is seen, wearing her red and white hospital ship colours, while undergoing routine repairs in the graving dock to the Todd Shipyards, at the Erie Basin, in Brooklyn, New York. Later, at the end of 1945, she was reconverted for trooping and then subsequently returned to the Italians.* (Victor Scrivens Collection.)

Above *The exquisite French* Normandie *had been laid up at New York since September 1939. Looked after by a small maintenance crew, her future was the subject of considerable speculation; from troop duties similar to the Cunard Queens to massive conversion to an aircraft carrier. She was officially seized by the US Government soon after the Japanese attack on Pearl Harbor, in December 1941, and officially renamed USS* Lafayette. *Stripped of her luxurious pre-war fittings and treasures, conversion to a 15,000-capacity trooper began at her berth, the French Line terminal at the foot of West 48th Street. Under a strong sense of urgency and with ensuing problems and carelessness, a small fire that quickly spread broke out aboard the ship on 9 February 1942. On that cold winter afternoon, mid-town Manhattan was soon covered in a thick blanket of orange-brown smoke. The* Normandie *was burning from end to end.* (Robert Russell Collection.)

Left *The* Normandie *fire was one of the war's saddest— and most embarrassing—tragedies. While the fire spread quickly and caused considerable damage, the ship might have been saved if it had not been for the chaotic, poorly planned firefighting methods. An armada of tugs and fireboats along with shoreside equipment poured tons of water onto the 1,028 ft long hull. In a blistering, smokey state, she gradually began to shift away from her berth, ripping mooring lines and tearing gangways.* (Robert Russell Collection.)

By the late afternoon of 9 February, the Normandie *fire was headline news. The curious descended on the waterfront; New Yorkers being able to see only the clouds of smoke overhead while, across the frozen Hudson, New Jerseyites lined the cliffs of the Palisades. Assuredly, it was one of the worst days that New York Harbor has ever known.* (Victor Scrivens Collection.)

In the dark, early morning hours of the 10 February, long after most spectators had departed and as fire crews were hopeful that the blaze would soon be extinguished, the 83,000-ton Normandie—*heavily overloaded with tons of water—rolled over and was lost forever. She settled in the murky, muddy waters of her slip, between Piers 88 (right) and 90. In the ice-filled waters of the Hudson River, she was a grotesque, horrifying, most pitiful sight. Salvage crews were immediately summoned for the most difficult task yet.* (Victor Scrivens Collection.)

The salvage of the Normandie *was the most difficult and tedious job of its kind ever undertaken, and required over twenty months and cost some £1.2 million ($5 million). In addition to eliminating the important use of two berths between Piers 88 and 90, a considerable section of the outer end of Pier 88 had to be dismantled and later rebuilt. A large catwalk was extended from the Pier across to the ship and a string of connected barges and floating derricks provided a temporary dock alongside the outer portion of the capsized ship. Systematically, her masts, funnels and upperworks were removed and scrapped. Divers worked within the ship where the original floors and decking were now bulkheads, and the port side bulkheads acted as floors. Sensibly, the Navy turned the project into an important diving school, possibly the only redemption to the loss of the* Normandie. *Pumps worked continuously until, in October 1943, the hulk was righted. Manoeuvred by a squadron of tugs, she was briefly drydocked, then laid-up and finally sold, in late 1945, to a local scrapper at Port Newark for a mere £40,000 ($161,000).*

In this exceptional photograph, the partial scrapping of the Normandie *is well underway. In wartime dress, the* Queen Mary's *forward section can be seen on the left; the aft portion of the* Queen Elizabeth *is on the right. (Robert Russell Collection.)*

An extraordinary view from the bridge of the capsized Normandie. *She is completely canted to port, a hopeless wreck of empty outer decks and tangled lines and rigging.* (Robert Russell Collection.)

By June 1945 the first troops began to return from the battlefields of Europe and later from the Far East. The liner-troopships, that had so vitally and urgently delivered millions to overseas posts, were now returning with masses of waving, cheering, often crying servicemen. Endless reunions took place at dockside. In the scene above, dated 11 July 1945, three tugs assist with the arrival of the USS West Point, *the former liner* America, *as she delivers over 7,500 soldiers to New York's Pier 86.* (Ernest Arroyo Collection.)

Chapter 4

The North Atlantic revisited

While in Nazi hands during the war, Norwegian America Line's *Stavangerfjord*, a 14,000-tonner, was barely touched and then left unharmed at the time of the liberation. Following some house-cleaning and fresh coats of paint, a crew was assembled and set off for New York, on the traditional run from Oslo, Copenhagen, Stavanger and Bergen, in August 1945. It was the first commercial liner crossing since the early war. It was also the beginning of a final boom period of Atlantic shipping, as shipping companies made millions, filled their ships to the very last upper berth and then used their profits to invest in new ships, more comfortable than ever before. It was also the final era of the transatlantic run. Within fifteen years of the *Stavangerfjord*'s historic passage, the jet had seized the majority of Atlantic travellers. The liners fell on hard times, then decline and finally withered into almost total disappearance.

The hard-pressed conditions of the immediate post-war years—unviable shipyards, shortages among workers and equipment, and even lingering financial woes—led many companies to conservative thinking. Only the Americans, who had previously had such a comparatively small share of the Atlantic trade, could even think of a big new supership. Others had to be content with more moderate replacement tonnage. The first new passenger ship to be launched after the hostilities, in September 1946, was a 12,000-tonner, a combination passenger-cargo ship for the Swedish American Line that would be named *Stockholm*. The first brand new passenger ship to enter service, in August 1947, was an untypical Cunarder; the 13,300-ton *Media*, another combination liner with space for a mere 250 passengers in all. Other firms were similarly cau-

tious or restrained. Canadian Pacific, which had lost the big 42,000-ton *Empress of Britain* during the early years of the war, would not think of new liners until the mid fifties, these being the 25,000-ton sisterships *Empress of Britain* and *Empress of England*. The French Line, left with only two adequate passenger ships, could only restore their luxury run between Le Havre and New York with the 17,000-ton *De Grasse*. She ran single-handedly for two years. In 1949, after a major refit, the magnificent pre-war *Ile de France* finally reappeared. The Holland-America Line, while needing a sistership or comparable running-mate for their highly popular *Nieuw Amsterdam* of 1938, would wait for nearly five years before adding new ships, namely a pair of the 15,000-tonners specially intended for the tourist and emigrant trades. The Germans were out of the running completely, until as late as 1954, while the Norwegians added the 16,800-ton *Oslofjord* by the end of 1949. The Mediterranean run was even more desolate. With much of their glorious pre-war fleet gone, the Italians slowly resurrected each of their four surviving liners, two of which went on the South American run while the other pair, the near-sisters *Saturnia* and *Vulcania*, normally employed on the Adriatic service out of Trieste and Venice, were deployed to the express run, from Genoa and Naples. While many of the sailings for all of these ships were filled to capacity, there was a noticeable lack of (or reluctance for) ordering new liners.

The Cunard Company was one of the first exceptions. Wanting a suitable companion to their 35,000-ton *Mauretania* of 1939, they commissioned the slightly smaller *Caronia* at the end of 1948. Her designs and intentions were reworked during the early stages of construction. While intended at the start to be a two-class transatlantic ship with wintertime capabilities for tropic cruising, her roles were reversed completely, in fact she would hardly spend any time on the Atlantic run whatsoever. She became the first major liner to be built with near year-round cruising in mind. It was a bold step by Cunard, in fact a very serious and clever insight into the future, especially as luxury cruising would one day, in well over a decade, replace the remains of the transatlantic trade. The *Caronia* was made to be exceptional; the largest single-stacker of her day, the tallest mast afloat, every cabin (for over 900 passengers) with private bathroom facilities and then painted overall in four distinctive shades of green. While most ships followed a set pattern of sailings that altered little from year to year, the *Caronia*'s standard was to go off on a three-month cruise around the world each winter, then to the Mediterranean in spring, the North Cape and Scandinavia in summer and finally a return to the Mediterranean in the autumn. It remains rather ironic that the first of the larger new post-war Atlantic liners was, in fact, designed as a cruiseship.

The American government became almost passionate about passenger liners after the war. They were certainly impressed with the blazing success of the converted Cunard Queens as they hauled as many as 15,000 soldiers per crossing. The government, while considerate of proud Yankee representation on the Atlantic Ferry, as the trade was often called, had very serious thoughts of using such new passenger ships, should the emergency arise, as high-capacity troopers. When building subsidies were offered to the American Export Lines, for a 29,000-ton pair that would be called the *Independence* and *Constitution*, an essential design element was the potential of easy conversion from 1,000 commercial berths to as many as 7,500 troops. High American technology was also incorporated in these ships, such as extra hull plating, elaborate engine rooms and an extensive use of aluminium.

While the *Independence* and *Constitution* were very fine entries to the transatlantic fleet, they were completely overshadowed a year or so after their commissioning by the most brilliant Atlantic supership of all time, the 53,300-ton *United States*. In July 1952, she swept the North Atlantic for the last time, taking the Blue Riband from the *Queen Mary* with an average speed of 36 kt. No ship, passenger or otherwise, has since exceeded her record. More importantly however, the sophisticated machinery aboard the new American flagship was such that an amazing 43 kt was recorded for a short sprint during the trial runs. A long, sleek liner, noticeably lower than most equivalent liners and with two enormous funnels atop her upper decks, the *United States* was the last ship to embody the concept of a 'seagoing greyhound.' Certainly her designers —using the theory that design affects speed— looked backward to such high performers as the *Normandie*, the *Bremen* and even the old *Mauretania* from 1907. Along with extra plating on the hull and an extreme sense of fire safety, the *United States* also had a double engine room while every pipe and wire had a twin duplicate. General safety and security, especially if under wartime attack, were paramount.

Frank Braynard, then a maritime reporter based at New York, was aboard the *United States* for her delivery voyage in June 1952: 'I saw her keel laid [8 February 1950], then saw her floated in drydock for the first time [23 June 1951] and sailed up with her on her delivery run, making her maiden arrival into New York in one of the port's most gala welcome occasions. She was the *United States*, the first American-built superliner of the 20th century, the world's safest ship and soon to prove herself the world's fastest. The trip, filled with the spirit of "Great Expectations", was one of the most thrilling experiences of my life. William Francis Gibbs [the ship's designer] was aboard with a host of maritime leaders and press. Spotless, shimmering, brand new and fantastic in evey respect, the new *United States* was America's dream ship. One reporter tested for vibration by putting a coin on its edge here and there from bow to stern. It never fell over. Others gathered in small groups and guessed at our speed. She would steam circles around the *Queen Mary*. And then the thunderous ovations as she entered New York port. What a moment! And best of all, the *United States* not only broke the Blue Riband record on her maiden voyage in both directions, but she went on to carry more passengers than any other Atlantic liner during her peak years of service.'

The *United States* headed a different and smaller breed of superships than had existed in the extravagance of the thirties. The two Cunard Queens were the most popular and successful team ever built, finally running that twin-ship transatlantic luxury shuttle between New York, Cherbourg and Southampton. Almost every Wednesday, at the New York end, one of the big Cunarders would sail, making the five-day passage mostly at 28½ kt. Their regularity was familiar to tens of thousands. Built of exceptional strength, they even worked their timetables in the most vicious of Atlantic weather; the blizzards, storms, mountainous waves, the crippling winds.

The Cunard fleet was the biggest on the North Atlantic in the mid fifties, heavily popularized by its apt slogan of 'Getting there is half the fun', and is reputed to have carried a third of all passengers that made the crossing. The Queens were, of course, the most popular. They offered three-class accommodation, topped by a superb first class that included sumptuous suites, precision service and the option of a three-deck high dining saloon or the more private Verandah Grill. Cabin class, termed the 'happy medium', offered spacious quarters that lacked the supposed 'stuffiness' of first class and the complete informality of tourist class. The tourist section, which was quite useful for budget tourists and emigrants, is surely the least remembered amidst the enduring legend of the Cunard Queens.

Cunard also ran the *Mauretania*, a 35,000-tonner that was as big as the Dutch flagship *Nieuw Amsterdam* and larger than any of the new Italian ships, on a supplementary service between Southampton, Le Havre, Cobh and New York. The motorliner *Britannic*, the last survivor from the White Star merger in the mid thirties, handled the Liverpool service with a call at Cobh in each direction. The *Caronia* made only periodic crossings, usually in preparation for one of her New York cruises. The combination passenger-cargo sisters *Media* and *Parthia*, a design unique to the Cunard fleet, sailed on a monthly rotation in direct service between Liverpool and New York. To the St Lawrence, Cunard maintained something of a secondary fleet. Several pre-war survivors, namely the *Samaria, Scythia, Franconia* and *Ascania*, soon gave way to a brand new quartet, the *Saxonia, Ivernia, Carinthia* and *Sylvania*. Cunard's peak year was 1957, with twelve liners trading on the North Atlantic.

The French Line rekindled much of its splendid pre-war reputation, deserved not only for their spectacular cuisine, but for their luxurious accommodation and meticulous service. No steamer company, transatlantic or otherwise, was more synonymous with red-suited bellboys, glistening champagne buckets and onion soup on the breakfast menu. Ada Louise Huxtable, in an article in *The New York Times* in 1980, wrote: 'The French Line had only one standard—the superlative. In the realm of the sybaritic, the French always seemed to do it best. Until its very last days, the liner *France* [commissioned in 1962 and then withdrawn in 1974] was considered the finest French restaurant in the world. The vin ordinaire was free, the cellars were a hushed treasury of rare vintages and the chefs leaped to anticipate the most epicurean demand.'

The *Ile de France*, having resumed luxury service in 1949, returned with almost the same decorative style that had made her such a favourite in the thirties. She was re-done in a late, Gallic version of Art Deco. Warehouses in France were ransacked and highly stylized chairs, sofas and tables found their away aboard the ship. Rich Aubusson carpets also went aboard as did some of the treasures saved from the magnificent *Normandie*. Just afterwards the French completed their transformation of the German *Europa*, given to them by the United Nations in 1946 as reparations for the *Normandie*, from a Teutonic flagship to Gallic luxury liner. Rechristened as the *Liberté* and reappearing in the summer of 1950, she became the perfect complement to the celebrated *Ile*. There were touches of latter day Art Deco, some streamlining and softening, some pieces from the *Normandie*, her own Café de l'Atlantique, a string of well furnished suites and apartments, and, of course, a superbly fed restaurant. The Cunard Queens, the *United States* and the two French liners were the most favoured of Atlantic ships in the fifties.

The Dutch, remaining quite conservative in nature until the mid fifties, added two otherwise important passenger ships in 1951–52. The sisterships *Ryndam* and *Maasdam*, originally intended to be sixty-passenger combination ships, were reworked in the earliest stages of construction and became 900-passenger 'tourist ships'. Carrying a mere 39 first class travellers in very top deck quarters, the 850 or so in the tourist class occupied an unparalleled 90 per cent of the ship's accommodation. Furthermore, it was the most comfortable tourist space at the time; a string of pleasant public rooms, a full restaurant, spacious outer decks and even an open-air swimming pool. With fares offered for as little as £7 4s ($20) per day (8 days to Cobh, 9 days to Southampton and Le Havre, etc), the appearance of these ships did nothing but revolutionize the Atlantic passenger trade. Tourist class dominance of accommodation soon spread to every new liner. As first and cabin class travellers began to desert the ships for airplanes and then the jets, the bulk of the trade, at least into the sixties, was the tourist class passenger.

The Italians began their rebuilding in the early fifties, first for their South American migrant trade and then, in 1953–54, for the more luxurious run to New York. While they had sailed the giant *Rex* and *Conte di Savoia* in the pre-war years, the directors in Genoa now saw superliners as unprofitable, bygone symbols of a lost era. Consequently, their new transatlantic flagships were the 29,000-ton sisters *Andrea Doria* and *Cristoforo Colombo*. The West Germans, still caught in the restrictions of post-war control, added their first passenger ship, the *Gripsholm* of 1925, which began sailing as the *Berlin* in 1955. The Swedes and the Norwegians, among the most seriously interested in a balanced trade of nine or so months on the Atlantic and the remainder in luxury cruising, opted for very contemporary ingredients of marine design. The *Kungsholm* of 1953 was the first North Atlantic liner to have all outside staterooms (certainly, a very useful feature for her off-season cruises as well) while the *Bergensfjord* of 1956 made extensive use of aluminium in her construction.

Other firms, wanting their share of the overflowing transatlantic profit, were content with second-hand ships. The Home Lines, based in Switzerland, with Italian staffing and partial Swedish financing, ran a string of converted liners. The Greek Line even employed two former Australian coastal steamers, both of them plodding their way westward with full loads of emigrants bound for either New York or Quebec City and Montreal. The Dutch Government, with the assistance of the Holland-America Line, ran a trio of converted wartime Victory ships that included, for their 800 passenger berths, dormitories with over 50 berths each. Certainly, the transatlantic trade in that final boom of the fifties catered for all budgets; from opulent suites on the *Liberté* complete with trunk rooms, dressing rooms, little dining rooms and even adjacent warming kitchens, to austere dormitory berths on small, converted aged ships.

As the Atlantic trade peaked, ports such as New York were often lined with passenger ships, offloading passengers, remaining at dock for several days and then outbound with a new set of travellers. City newspapers often published photographs of great gatherings of liners, especially the larger ships, as they were berthed in orderly formation along the West Side piers known as 'Luxury Liner Row'. The arrival schedules, published in both the *Herald Tribune* and *The New York Times*, presented abundant lists, such as the week's list below from September 1950:

Ship & number of passengers	From	Pier
Monday 4 September		
Argentina [364]	Buenos Aires	Canal Street
Jamaica [97]	Puerto Barrois	Morris Street
Puerto Rico [115]	San Juan	Pacific Street, Brooklyn
Santa Isabel [38]	Valparaiso	West 16th Street
Tuesday 5 September		
Queen Elizabeth [2,224]	Southampton	West 50th Street
Italia [1,152]	Lisbon	West 14th Street
Mauretania [1,135]	Southampton	West 50th Street
Vulcania [1,472]	Naples	West 44th Street
Erria [94]	Copenhagen	8th Street, Hoboken
Queen of Bermuda	Bermuda	West 55th Street
Santa Sofia	Barranquilla	West 10th Street
Wednesday 6 September		
America	Southampton	West 21st Street
Fort Townshend	Halifax	West 55th Street
Panama	Cristobal	West 24th Street
Santa Rosa	Cartagena	West 16th Street
Thursday 7 September		
Batory [829]	Gdynia	West 48th Street
Friday 8 September		
Washington	Southampton	West 21st Street
Saturday 9 September		
Caronia	Southampton	West 50th Street
Parthia	Liverpool	West 14th Street
De Grasse	Le Havre	West 48th Street
Sunday 10 September		
Roma	Cherbourg	4th Street, Hoboken

The liners came and went with familiar regularity and have left strong impressions on tourists, waterfront artists, ship enthusiasts and, in particular, motorists along the old West Side Highway, which was placed alongside the largest luxury liner docks at New York. Drivers would pause momentarily, gazing at the extraordinary groupings of as many as ten liners at one time. The ships, resting between voyages, would sit in unhurried splendour; their sharp bows pointed against the inner bulkheads, the towering masts so gracefully tilted, the pure white upper decks and as many as three enormous funnels. Richard Morse recalled a more memorable day, 3 July 1956:

'During vacation, I made one of the Circle Line cruises around Manhattan island. The absolute high point was, however, to see the *Queen Mary, Caronia, Liberté, United States, America* and *Andrea Doria* all in a row! It was the height of the eastbound transatlantic season. Unfortunately, fate had decreed that this would be the last time New York would see the *Andrea Doria*. [She sank off Nantucket, on 26 July, after colliding with the Swedish *Stockholm*.]

'That evening, I went aboard the *Liberté* for a visit. Both she and the *Caronia* were due to sail at 11 pm. The *Liberté* would be off on a transatlantic crossing and the *Caronia* on a North Cape cruise. I thoroughly enjoyed exploring the *Liberté*'s first class accommodations including the celebrated Café de l'Atlantique, dining salon, main lounge, theatre, chapel, etc. I had a fill of Gallic charm and style, not forgetting to examine closely the items which had been saved from the *Normandie*. After all, this was *the* flagship of the French Line! My peregrinations tired me out and so I found a chair on the sports deck abaft the second funnel, where I took it all in, pretending that we were already in mid-Atlantic, enjoying the delights of the Compagnie Générale Transatlantique.

'Presently, a frightful bellow was heard, indicating to one and all that sailing time was imminent. The *Liberté* had a couple of steam horns that really commanded respect; the E and C sharp two octaves below middle C. In that way, she was in a class with the *United States* and the two Queens. Of course, none of them could make the 'Gates of Hell' sound of the *Ile de France*! I had heard sound off, along with the *Constitution* and *Stockholm*, just the previous Saturday.

'I scampered off to the pier, went out on the terrace and watched the *Liberté* back out into the mid-Hudson darkness. It was an unforgettable sight. She was lit up like a Christmas tree, her giant stacks illuminated and her name emblazoned on both sides like some sort of advertisement. After she got into mid-river, she turned seaward and proceeded to wait for the *Caronia* to depart. Then, forming a team, they sailed down the Hudson in all their majesty. The *Queen Mary, United States, America* and *Andrea Doria* were left behind to spend Independence Day in New York Harbor.

'I returned to the docks on Saturday to see the *America* and the *Conte Biancamano*. Indeed, it was an interesting first week in July!'

In addition to newspaper photographs of the liners at dock, there were also frequent scenes of celebrities onboard. Assuredly, the most recorded were the Windsors, usually seen as they entered a gangplank with several dogs in tow. Others included Hollywood film queens like Ava Gardner, Lana Turner, Rita Hayworth and Elizabeth Taylor. Then, there would be figures from politics, Winston Churchill, Dwight Eisenhower, Queen Frederika of Greece and President Tito of Yugoslavia. Until the decline of the transatlantic liners at New York, reporters customarily met the inbound ships in a launch in the outer reaches of the harbour. They would climb aboard and have several hours prior to actual disembarkation to interview and photograph the more famous passengers. One rather amusing tale from this era concerns actress Greta Garbo, the most secretive and consequently sought-after of the film queens of the twenties and thirties. Henry Luce, the chairman of the Time-Life Incorporated, learned that Garbo was inbound from Europe on the *Liberté*. He summoned as many as a hundred reporters to his offices and promised a lifetime job to the reporter that could manage an interview with the reclusive Swede. On the day of arrival, the reporters sailed out to meet the ship and then climbed aboard. All but one searched through the public rooms, assuming that even Garbo had to pass through immigration and passport formalities. That lone reporter, with the help of a well-tipped steward, located her cabin, a rather unpretentious first class single. Posting himself outside the door, his patience seemed to be rewarded when a woman, dressed in dark glasses and floppy hat, came running along the corridor. It was, of course, Garbo who was by then aware of the upper deck reporters. While Garbo fumbled with her cabin key, she brushed alongside the waiting reporter and excused herself with a simple 'Pardon'. It was the only word that Garbo did, in fact, say to any of the press on that day. That enterprising reporter returned to shore, wrote an entire story on his 'One Word Interview with Garbo', and landed the job with Henry Luce.

The days of first class celebrities, crowded main lounges, walks around the promenade deck and, more importantly, full rosters of passengers were coming to a close by the late fifties. As the first commercial jet crossed in 1958, the airlines secured nearly two-thirds of the total transoceanic traffic within six months. Many steamship companies, particularly in the closed settings of their boardrooms, tended at first to ignore this new competitor. One director at Cunard responded, 'Flying is but a fad. There will always be passengers to fill ships like the grand *Queen Mary*.' It was a sad, very sad miscalculation. By 1961, both Queens along with the brilliant *United States* began to slip further and further into the red. As peak summer season sailings slipped, mid-winter voyages were all but deserted. The 640-passenger *Oslofjord* reached New York in December with a scant sixty passengers aboard while the 1,348-passenger *Leonardo da Vinci* left Naples with a mere 200 on her lists.

It was difficult at first to accept the cruel reality that the transatlantic liner trade was finished, what was to become of the existing companies and their ships? In the decade that began in the mid sixties all but Cunard, with that well publicized last survivor, the *Queen Elizabeth 2*, pulled out. The Americans, so reliant on government subsidies, were the first notable loss. The handsome *America*, the 33,500-ton companion to the *United States*, found new life with the Greeks, on the Australian migrant trade as the *Australis*. Her capacity was doubled, from 1,046 to 2,258. The *Independence* and *Constitution* soon followed, after a misguided attempt to convert them for Caribbean cruising. They spent years at backwater berths awaiting buyers. Once cleared for foreign flag use, they went to the gigantic C. Y. Tung Group of Hong Kong, with whom they were eventually reactivated as Hawaiian cruiseships. The *United States* closed out Yankee service on the Atlantic in the autumn of 1969. At the onset of yet another disruptive, costly strike, her owners returned the ship to the government, her mortgage holder. For well over a decade she sat at an unused finger pier at Norfolk, not very far from her birthplace at Newport News, the subject of myriads of part truths and rumours, from conversion to a floating missionary church to use as a floating motel. Bought by Seattle interests in 1978, she was drydocked for the first time two years later. Little else followed for some time. By early 1985, press reports are that she will be rebuilt, partially in a German shipyard as well as by an American company, with 1,200 one-class berths for cruising. Preliminary advertising has called the project 'the rebirth of a transatlantic legend.'

While the *Ile de France* and *Liberté* went to the boneyards after long, very successful and prestigious lives, the 66,300-ton *France*, commissioned as the 'last liner designed almost totally for the Atlantic', in as late as 1962, had slightly over a decade of service. That superb image of the French Line and its quality of service and food remained intact, but while the liner was profitable in numbers (she rarely slipped below 90

per cent occupancy), she was financially ailing. Each season she required larger, more expensive subsidies—even when filled to the very last upper berth in tourist class. In the late summer of 1974, French government officials announced that the subsidy moneys would be better used, offering richer prestige in a more technological world, for the supersonic Concorde. The *France*, still in mint condition, was abruptly withdrawn and quietly sat out the next five years at a lonely backwater berth at Le Havre. Bought by the Norwegians in 1979, she has been reactivated, in the most successful conversion of all former Atlantic liners, from the 'indoor' *France* to the 'outdoor' *Norway*.

Cunard, with the largest transatlantic liner fleet, even in the twilight years, was perhaps hardest hit. However, they seemed to present stubborn refusal that the jet was victorious. By 1965, dramatic changes were in order, especially if the company was to survive. Alone, the Queens were losing near to £1.5 million a year. Consequently within three years, between 1965 and 1968, Cunard retired the *Mauretania, Queen Mary, Caronia, Carinthia, Sylvania* and *Queen Elizabeth*, and then converted the only survivors, the *Carmania* and *Franconia*, into cruiseships. Sensibly they had revised the order for their new superliner, a 65,000-tonner that was building on the Clyde, to spend about half her year as a twin-class transatlantic ship and the remainder as a one-class cruiseship. In fact, almost from the start, the Atlantic crossings for this ship, the *Queen Elizabeth 2*, reflect more of a cruiseship atmosphere than the quieter, more conservative, class-divided tone of the earlier ships. Transport has been replaced by sea-going fun and enjoyment as the major objectives of passenger ship firms.

The last major company to withdraw was the Italian Line in as late as 1976. Long deficit-ridden, but kept alive by huge subsidies from Rome that were prodded on by powerful seamen's unions, the Italian fleet also had a sad decline. When the *Giulio Cesare* developed mechanical problems in 1972, there was little effort to repair her. Instead, she was sent to the scrappers. The *Cristoforo Colombo*, after a brief reprieve on the South American run, finished her days as a hotel ship for workers at the steel plants along the Orinoco River at Mantanzas. The *Augustus* was sold off to unknown Far Eastern buyers and has since been moving from anchorage to anchorage without purpose. The *Michelangelo* and *Raffaello*, superships constructed in as late as 1965 and which never earned a profit, finished ten years of service only. They were eventually sold to the Shah of Iran's government, who wanted them as permanently moored army barracks. The *Michelangelo* went to Bandar Abbas, the *Raffaello* to Bushire. Long neglected and all but abandoned, the *Raffaello* was sunk during an Iraqi air attack in early 1983. Finally, the *Leonardo da Vinci*, which made the last Italian transatlantic crosing, lingered for a short time as a Florida-based cruiseship. Suffering from financial woes, including an increasing hunger for expensive fuel oils, she was later retired, but amidst further prodding by the seamen's unions to reactivate her. Considerable debate followed, but finally ended when, in July 1980, the *Leonardo da Vinci* mysteriously caught fire while at an unmanned anchorage. She

burned out for several days and finally capsized, another blackened corpse resembling those ruined Italian liners of the thirties that were destroyed in the war. The story of another Atlantic 'dinosaur' had finished.

The *Queen Elizabeth 2* is the last survivor of the old traditional service. Ironically, she is said to be more profitable on her Atlantic crossings than as an off-season cruiseship. The dozen or so voyages scheduled each year are filled largely by nostalgic travellers wanting to sample the 'grand life', that lost age of transatlantic ocean liner travel. (One further ship, Poland's *Stefan Batory*, crosses out of Montreal. Now aged, her days are numbered and her position in passenger ship annals not quite the same as for that last big Cunarder.)

Below left *As the hostilities ended, many converted liners continued in troop service for at least another year. Almost in equal numbers, millions of military personnel had to be returned to their homelands. Once Government service ended, however, the restoration and rejuventation plans quickly got underway. In themselves, these were extraordinary undertakings, often more complicated than the original construction. There were post-war shortages of berths, craft workers and artisans, machinery and even small items such as door hinges. Undoubtedly, the biggest transformations were with the Cunard Queens. The* Queen Elizabeth *was released in March 1946, and then, at an anchorage at the mouth of the River Clyde in Scotland, she was stripped, overhauled and then partially refitted. Too large to proceed upriver to her original building berth at the John Brown Yards, she was worked on in the outer harbour, fed by a steady succession of tugs, barges and repair boats. The project was completed at Southampton, where the final fittings—such as the furnishings and artwork— went aboard. She was gloriously commissioned for her first commercial service, having missed her intended maiden voyage in April 1940, in October 1946. As seen here, the* Queen Mary *returned to Southampton on her last trooping voyage in September 1946. Then she too was totally restored, with all of the work being done at the Southampton Docks, and reappeared on the North Atlantic in commercial dress in the summer of 1947.* (Frank O. Braynard Collection.)

Right *While many of the surviving Nazi German liners were sunk in the final months of the war, the few remaining ships—often left in very poor condition—were taken as prizes by the invading Allied forces. Hamburg America Line's* Milwaukee, *a transatlantic and then popular cruise liner from the thirties, had been used as a naval accommodation ship at Kiel from 1940. She was taken as a British war prize, on 9 May 1945, and briefly reactivated as the troopship* Empire Waveney. *In the following March, while undergoing a much needed refit at Liverpool, she caught fire, burnt out completely and then heeled over and sank. Of little value thereafter, she was raised and then towed to Glasgow for scrapping.* (Richard K. Morse Collection.)

Above left *The greatest war prize of all surviving German liners was, in fact, the third largest ship then afloat, the 49,700-ton* Europa. *Owned by the North German Lloyd, a one-time Blue Riband record breaker but then never used during the war, she was found to be in very poor condition by her American captors. The Nazis had hoped to use her (and her near-sister* Bremen, *which burned in 1941) for their intended sea invasion of Britain. After some hurried repairs, the US Navy reactivated the ship, her first time at sea in over five years, in September 1945. Well loaded with over 5,000 soldiers and crew, she steamed for New York. Unfortunately, over the next months, the USS* Europa *was plagued by continuous, quite serious fires. She was soon given over to the United Nations for reparations assignment and then assigned to the French, in compensation for the loss of the* Normandie. *After considerable restoration and alteration, the* Europa *would reappear on the North Atlantic luxury trade as the* Liberté. *(Victor Scrivens Collection.)*

Above right *From that summer of 1947 until the retirement of the* Queen Mary *in 1967, the two giant Cunard Queens ran the most prestigious, impeccable superliner express run of all time. While originally intended to have started in April 1940, but then disrupted by the outbreak of the war, it was the first twin-liner express ever. Previously, all of the major routes on the North Atlantic required at least three major ships: Cunard's* Aquitania, Berengaria *and* Mauretania; *White Star's* Majestic, Olympic *and* Homeric; *and North German Lloyd's* Bremen, Europa *and* Columbus.

The Queens ran their weekly service, with 28 kt runs, in relays between New York and Southampton and with a call at Cherbourg in each direction. Their only deviations to this pattern for most of their lives were their annual winter overhauls at Southampton each winter and then brief maintenance dry docking in midsummer. As the Queen Mary *left Southampton on Thursday, the* Queen Elizabeth *was already outbound from New York, having departed on Wednesday. On the following week, the* Elizabeth *reached Southampton on Monday and the* Mary *at New York on Tuesday. The process was then reversed and rotated continuously. It was the ideal balance in luxury passenger shipping, a process that was familiar to and popular with millions. (Everett Viez Collection.)*

While the Queens had a most magnificent record for precision arrivals and sailings, the two ships were not without their occasional mishaps and problems. The Queen Elizabeth *went aground in the approaches to the Solent, at Southampton, on 14 April 1947. With 2,246 passengers and considerable cargo aboard, she was 'locked' in position for nearly a day, and floated off only to be delayed further by a thick fog. The* Queen Mary *went aground off Cherbourg two years later, in January 1949. She had to make an emergency return to Southampton, where some 100 tons of concrete were put in her dented stern as temporary repairs. Some years later, in March 1956, the* Queen Mary *was so violently tossed about in a huge Atlantic storm that forty passengers and fifty crew were injured. In August 1959, in a thick summer's haze, the* Queen Elizabeth *grazed the freighter* American Hunter *in the outer reaches of New York Harbor and then had to return to port for inspection. Fire was another dreaded possibility. The* Queen Elizabeth *was nearly destroyed on 8 March 1946, just after being decommissioned from war service at Southampton. It took three hours to control the upper-deck blaze. In September 1960, while approaching the English Channel, three of her first class staterooms were damaged by fire caused by faulty electrical wiring.*

This photograph shows Queen Mary *being manoeuvred by tugs in Southampton, October 1948. (Frank O. Braynard Collection.)*

Left *Because of their considerable draft, placed at over 38 ft for each ship, the* Queens *were forced to move with the tides. Therefore, their arrival and sailing times were constantly changing. On one week, the Queen Mary would arrive at New York on Tuesday at 12.00 and then sail at 11.00 on Wednesday. The following week, the Queen Elizabeth would arrive at 08.00 on Tuesday and then depart at 16.30 on the Wednesday. Of course, the most tender and often well-publicized of all arrivals or departures were during the strikes among the tugboats. Upon arrival, these giants would specially reduce speed as they passed along the Hudson to their midtown berth at Pier 90. The captains and their officers, being pushed to their limit of their skills, cautiously approached the 1,100 ft finger pier. Some of the ship's lifeboats might be lowered into the Hudson to guide the ships and then relay some of the mooring lines to the dockers. While the normal berthing of one of the* Queens *averaged 35 minutes, it might take as much as three hours during a tug strike.* (Port Authority of New York & New Jersey.)

Below *Aside from their distinctions as the world's largest liner (the* Queen Elizabeth*) and the world's fastest until 1952 (the* Queen Mary*), the* Queens *were perhaps most publicized for the celebrities they transported. Newspaper and magazine photographs often featured deck scenes, a customary life ring in position, with a posed starlet, politician or aristocrat in place. Churchill crossed on the* Queen Mary *to New York in late 1951, travelling with a staff of forty. The Duke and Duchess of Windsor were constant patrons until they changed loyalties to the new* United States *in 1952. The Queen Mother sailed in the* Queen Elizabeth *in October 1954, the ship she had named at the ship's launching in September 1938, and then returned from New York aboard the* Queen Mary *a month later. Noel Coward once complained of meeting 'too many celebrities' aboard the* Queens.

The moodful photograph shows a departing Queen Elizabeth, *outbound after a two-week strike at Southampton, in December 1948. On that same day, with schedules in disorder, the* Queen Mary *and* Aquitania *sailed as well.* (Frank O. Braynard Collection.)

Above *At New York, well into the 1960s, the trans-atlantic liners generally arrived in the very early morning hours, just after the first daylight, their first passengers going ashore just after breakfast. In this dramatic aerial view of the Hudson River, with the curving shape of Manhattan island so clearly visible, three major liners are inbound. Just below the American Export liner* Constitution, *which is already berthed at Pier 84, the Blue Ribband champion* United States *is being guided by Moran tugboats into the north slip of Pier 86. She has just arrived from Southampton, Le Havre and Bremerhaven. The Italian* Cristoforo Colombo *is slowly approaching her designated berth, the south side of Pier 84, just across from the* Constitution. *The* Cristoforo Colombo *is inbound from Gibraltar, Cannes, Genoa and Naples. Further down river, in midstream and not yet having collected her tugs, the majestic* Queen Mary *is returning from her five-day crossing from Cherbourg and Southampton. One other liner, placed well along the Manhattan West Side docks, is already docked as well. She is the Norwegian-America Line's* Oslofjord, *having arrived from Copenhagen, Bergen, Stavanger and Oslo. (Port Authority of New York & New Jersey.)*

Right *The liners were especially graceful and photogenic as they sailed along the Hudson River at New York. In this helicopter view, Italy's brand new flagship, the 33,300-ton* Leonardo da Vinci, *is receiving a gala escort for her maiden arrival. The time is an early Saturday morning in the summer of 1960. Built to replace the ill-fated* Andrea Doria, *which sank off Natucket four years before, the 761 ft long* Leonardo da Vinci—*if placed on end—would be almost as high as the sixty-storey Woolworth Tower, once the tallest office building in the world, which can be seen just to the right of centre in this photograph. (Sal Scannella Collection.)*

Coincidental gatherings of the great ocean liners were frequent at New York, especially along 'Luxury Liner Row', the 1,100 ft long finger piers that stretched from West 44th to West 52nd Streets. Two additional, but much smaller berths, Piers 95 and 97, at West 55th and 57th Street, were also included. Newspaper centrefolds often carried impressive aerial photos of these groupings, under such headline captions as the 'superships at the super piers'. In this wintery view, dated 6 December 1957, no less than nine liners are in port together. Looking northward, American Export's Independence *and then the Italian Line's* Augustus *share Pier 84; the United States Lines' running-mates* America *and* United States *follow at Pier 86; the French Line's* Liberte, *at Pier 88, is just above the American flagship; Cunard's* Queen Elizabeth *is at Pier 90 and followed by the combination liner* Media; *and at the top, almost obscured, is the Furness-Bermuda Line cruiseships* Ocean Monarch *and finally North German Lloyd's* Berlin. *(Port Authority of New York & New Jersey.)*

Several years later, on another winter afternoon, six major liners are captured by a clever cameraman. Dated 13 February 1962, it is, in fact a special occasion—the first departure of the brand new superliner France, *which is just about to sail from her berth at Pier 88. Despite the obvious cold and gusty winds that sweep in off the Hudson River, crowds are lining the inner bulkhead of the slip as well as the outer-end verandah. Other ships include the Italian Line's* Cristoforo Colombo *in the top position, berthed on the north side of Pier 84; the* America *and then the* United States *sharing Pier 86; the* France; *and finally Cunard's* Ivernia *and the Greek Line's* Olympia *together at Pier 90. (Richard K. Morse Collection.)*

Amidst the high pitch of the post-war years, new and often innovative liners appeared each year. Some were built to replace war losses, others to supplement existing fleets and still others as completely new endeavours. Unquestionably, the most important, noteworthy and stunning of this new generation was the superliner United States. She swept the seas forever, the last holder of the coveted Blue Riband. Begun with preliminary designs at the height of the war, in 1943, she was intended to be a high performance peacetime commercial profit maker, but easily convertible to a wartime trooper with at least 15,000 berths. This latter dimension was, of course, inspired heavily by the blazing success of the two big Cunard Queens as high-capacity, speeding troopships. The keel plates for this American flagship were laid down in February 1950, and—in almost extraordinary time for a superliner—she was 'floated' (rather than launched) for the first time little more than fifteen months later. (United States Lines.)

During her maiden voyage from New York to Le Havre and Southampton, in July 1952, the United States took the Blue Riband from the Queen Mary. The Cunarder's best speed was 31.6 kts; the new American had an average of over 35 kts. She was a full 5 kts or ten hours better than her British predecessor. Long and sleek, with two enormous red, white and blue funnels, the 'American beauty', as she was sometimes called, was a futuristic ship in many respects. She had the greatest use of aluminium built into her construction of any liner around; every system—mechanical, electrical and plumbing—had a twin duplicate; her fire safety provisions were exceptional the only wood onboard was said to be in the piano and butcher's block; and her twin, top-secret engine rooms were later reported to have produced speeds of some 43 knots. For her first decade on the North Atlantic, and despite the obvious lack of an equivalent running-mate so as to run weekly sailings in each direction, the United States—also known as the 'Big U'—was the most popular major liner in the trade. (Everett Viez Collection.)

The running-mate to the United States was the smaller, slower America, completed in 1940 and, in fact, a prototype to the larger speed queen. However, many passengers did prefer this more moderate ship. Her interior was said to be more comfortable and snug, her overall numbers fewer and many travellers actually enjoyed the additional time at sea. Whereas the United States made Le Havre and Southampton in a flat five days, the America sailed to Cobh in six, to Le Havre and Southampton in seven and then to Bremerhaven in eight.

In this scene, captured from the America's starboard bridge wing, the liner is inbound at New York on a moody, misty morning. A Moran tug has come alongside, about to deliver the docking pilot, who will complete the ship's transatlantic passage. (Fred Rodriguez Collection.)

Amidst special enthusiasm for large ocean liners, especially considering their deliberately designed adaptability to emergency troop transports, the American Government, in the form of the American Export Lines, added two superb 29,000-tonners in 1951. Appropriately named Independence (shown here as she approaches Naples, with Mount Vesuvius in the background) and Constitution, they were very strong and serious competitors to the Italian Line, which had long dominated the transatlantic trade to the Mediterranean. The Yankee pair, working balanced tandem sailings, sailed the aptly named 'Sunlane Route' on three-week round trips to Algeciras, Naples, Genoa, Cannes and then homeward via Algeciras again. A notable alteration occurred in 1956, however, when the Constitution was diverted to Monte Carlo to deliver actress Grace Kelly to her wedding to the local prince. (Everett Viez Collection.)

Transatlantic passages of a week or longer, such as aboard Holland-America's beloved Nieuw Amsterdam, *were uneventful passages by today's busy cruiseship standards. Days were unhurried and restful. There were long hours mostly in sheltered deckchairs, a good book often in hand. There would be bouillon at eleven and tea at four. A film might be shown in mid-afternoon, but more likely would be featured as an after-dinner diversion. Other night-time events would be horse-racing, using those white-coloured wooden mounts that were guided by attendant stewards, a spirited game of bingo or possibly some dancing music, using just a phonograph on the smaller ships. Until the early and mid sixties, the transatlantic liners were primarily interested in providing safe, comfortable and reliable transport across the Atlantic. Only in latter years, when prodded by jetcraft competition and then by the appearance of sleek, trendy cruiseships, did the remaining transatlantic ships seem to embellish their daily programmes and 'floating resort' qualities. (Captain Cornelius van Herk Collection.)*

Calm, tranquil passages were often less memorable. This poetic scene, of a sunlit sea on a late afternoon, was taken by Everett Viez aboard the Queen Mary, *west-bound from Cherbourg to New York, on 27 October 1956. Alternatively, no matter how disruptive or alarming, it seems to be the storm-tossed, battered crossings that linger most in the memory. Covered portholes, specially secured furniture and those specially erected ropelines in foyers and lounges often remain as details. Even the biggest liners might be delayed by as much as 48 hours. There were, of course, the more serious occasions; the storm-dented superstructure aboard the* Ile de France, *the string of broken promenade deck windows on the* Bremen *and—perhaps worst of all—the punctured forward decks and washed-out cabins aboard the* Michaelangelo. *(Everett Viez Collection.)*

While some lines began to detour to more tranquil, sunny and profitable cruise routes to the Caribbean and Mediterranean, some liners persisted with their transatlantic schedules even in the depths of bitter winter. Gusty winds, biting temperatures, a thick salt spray and ice-encrusted decks, lifeboats and rigging fill out this view of the Home Lines' Italia during a December crossing in the mid fifties between Hamburg, the Channel ports, Halifax and New York. (Everett Viez Collection.)

Outbound from New York for Southampton and Le Havre, the great bow section of the 936-ft Liberté is covered in ice as she prepared for her voyage to the open Atlantic. Chilling winds and frigid temperatures made the departure process most difficult. Few visitors crowded on to the open-deck pierside verandahs to wave these sailings off. On board, overcoated or fur-wrapped passengers huddled behind those long rows of promenade deck windows. A handful of broad-shouldered officers might be seen peering down from the open bridge wings above and as a few deckhands relinquished the final lines to humble little tugs such as the Eugene F. Moran. Patient and skilled photographers, such as Allan Liddy of the Flying Camera Company which recorded the movements of so many ships at New York, deserve high praises for their excellent work under such bleak conditions. (Fred Rodriguez Collection.)

The new generation of post-war liners on the North Atlantic included some of the most interesting and innovative ships of all time. The Cunard Company, for example, ordered a sizable ship in 1946, the first major British liner to be built after the war, as a running-mate of sorts to their pre-war Mauretania of 1939. The new ship was not even a near-sister, however. She was totally novel and unique in purpose. When completed at the end of 1948 the Caronia, at over 34,000 tons and 715 ft in length and was then by far the biggest liner yet built that would spend most of her year in luxury, all-first-class cruising. In fact, she would make only occasional appearances on the North Atlantic shuttle. Painted overall in four very distinctive, eye-catching shades of green, she soon developed an established pattern: Around the world or an equally long cruise each January; the Mediterranean in spring; Scandinavia in summer; and a return to the Mediterranean in the autumn. In design annals, the new Cunarder represented several other trends of the future: a large, single stack instead of the customary two or three, a tall mast placed above the bridge and every passenger cabin, regardless of class (she could carry first and cabin class passengers for Atlantic crossings), fitted with private bathroom facilities. In this scene the Caronia is arriving at New York, on 19 January 1956, in preparation for her world cruise departure. In the background are four other British liners; Canadian Pacific's Empress of Scotland to the left and then three Cunarders just behind the Caronia, the Franconia, Mauretania and Queen Mary. (Richard K. Morse Collection.)

The Holland-America Line revolutionized comfortable tourist class travel in the early fifties with two brand new liners, the sisters Ryndam (shown here) and Maasdam. For the first time in the Atlantic liner travel, the tourist class quarters occupied the best and better parts of the ship. First class, with a scant 39 berths, was arranged in an upper-deck penthouse section. Alternately, the 822 passengers in the tourist section, with daily fares beginning as low as £7 ($20), had large lounges, an attractive dining room, an outdoor pool and the greatest open-air deck spaces. In quick time, with considerable refinement and improvement, tourist class dominance spread to many other transatlantic companies. (Captain Cornelius van Herk Collection.)

Above *While companies such as Holland-America continued with other basically tourist class passenger ships, a revived era of the 'ships of state', so similar to the thirties, took hold in the late fifties. Ironically, it came just as the jet made its first commercial flight (in October 1958) and began its conquest. However, most of these new ships enjoyed several years of popularity and success, and then were quite sensibly shifted to the tropical, one-class cruise trades as an alternative. Like others, the Dutch built a new national flagship, the 38,600-ton Rotterdam, completed in the late summer of 1959. Exquisitely furnished with examples of national art, craftsmanship and technology, she had one very noticeable distinction. She was the first major liner on the Atlantic to do away with the conventional smokestack. Instead, her exhausts were worked through twin upstakes placed aft.* (Port Authority of New York & New Jersey.)

Left *The new Italian 'ship of state', another national flagship of brilliance, was the Leonardo da Vinci of 1960. Expressly designed for the very popular sunshine route to the Mediterranean, her outer decks included no less than five swimming pools, including one that was infra-red heated for cooler weather. However, masked behind a rather conventional appearance of a single stack and mast, and propelled by quite ordinary steam turbines, the Leonardo da Vinci's designers looked ahead to future years. There was considerable provision for conversion to nuclear power.* (Port Authority of New York & New Jersey.)

Right *One of the most popular and friendly of the new generation of 'tourist liners', the French Line's Flandre of 1952, had one of the most embarassing maiden arrivals at New York. During her first westbound crossing, she was crippled by electrical and mechanical failures. When she reached New York, she had to be towed to her berth at Pier 88 during the traditional fireboat reception. The French were mortified while the local dockers did little to sympathize with the dilemma by referring to the new ship as 'the Flounder'. (Port Authority of New York & New Jersey.)*

Below *Later, with her mechanical woes long behind, the Flandre is shown outbound from New York, on 16 August 1962, alongside the Atlantic's oldest liner at the time, the 44-year-old Stavangerfjord of the Norwegian America Line. She endured beyond all expectations and was a beloved favourite until her final voyage a year later, in December. Built during the First World War, the early era charms of her quarters enchanted many travellers. In the contemporary age of stainless steels and veneers, formicas and vinyls, the wood panels and gilded columns of a ship such as the Stavangerfjord seemed to represent a lost era. Like several other very popular Atlantic liners, there were proposals put forth to save them in the end. The Norwegians wanted to make a cadet training ship or a floating hostel or even a maritime museum. The best bid came, however, from Hong Kong scrappers. (Richard K. Morse Collection.)*

The French Line's Ile de France *was one of the greatest and grandest liners of all. Consequently, when she was finally retired in late 1958, after 31 years of distinguished service, her owners wished for a gentle, peaceful ending in the solitude of a Japanese scrapyard. Of course, she too was the subject of schemes for survival; a floating hotel, a casino and again a museum ship. Such ideas, while attractive and sentimental, are mostly unsuccessful and expensive. However, after the* Ile de France *was sold to the Osaka breakers, she was temporarily leased to a Hollywood film company to be systematically blasted, wrecked and partially sunk on film. Her former owners were shocked. In future, as with the sale of another 31-year-old liner the* Liberte (*shown here*)*, in 1961, to Italian scrappers, there were strict contractual clauses forbidding such misuse of legendary ships.* (French Line.)

Those veteran French liners, the Ile de France *and* Liberte, *were replaced by the North Atlantic's last purposely-built express liner, the 66,300-ton* France *of 1962. Highly styled, beautifully served and brilliantly fed, she was, in fact, too late to be a large financial success as well. The jet had taken a firm hold on the trade, leaving less than ten per cent of the total traffic for passenger ships by the mid sixties. Instead, and while mostly filled to the very last upper berth, the* France *was supported by Government subsidy. Like her earlier predecessors, particularly the* Normandie, *her profits were measured in national prestige. The financial aspects were seemingly irrelevant, at least for some years.*

In this night time view, taken in February 1970, the 1,035 ft long France—*the longest liner of all—is still at berth as the glowing Italian* Michelangelo *departs on a Caribbean cruise.* (French Line.)

Sisterships or the teams of great liners were rarely to be seen in port together. On those odd occasions when they were together it was often recorded and featured in newspapers and magazines as a special event. In this scene, on 16 October 1959, the two largest Dutch liners, Holland America's Rotterdam *(lower ship)* and Nieuw Amsterdam are 'ping ponging', exchanging berths, at their Hoboken terminal. Since only one slip was capable of handling such large ships, the Rotterdam had to be temporarily moved to a cargo pier while the Nieuw Amsterdam arrived, offloaded and then reloaded passengers. It was a busy swap for the harbour tugs. (Richard K. Morse Collection.)

Running-mates, such as Norwegian America's Oslofjord *(left)* and Bergensfjord, *often appeared to be exact sisterships. These ships, used on the run to Copenhagen, Bergen, Stavanger and Oslo, were very similar in design, which included the same tapered single funnels. However, the* Oslofjord, *built in 1949, was the slightly smaller, with a lower capacity and more cargo space. Alternately, the* Bergensfjord, *commissioned seven years later, in 1956, had a more extended superstructure, larger passenger quarters and less cargo space.*

Similarly, however, both ships—like many others in the fifties and sixties—began to divide their time between peak tourist summers on the traditional Atlantic routes and then winters on all-first-class cruises. Along with shorter runs to Bermuda, Nassau and the Caribbean, both Norwegian liners were well known for their longer, more luxurious jaunts; around the world, circle Pacific, around South America, the Mediterranean and the North Cape. (Richard K. Morse Collection.)

Above left *Each winter, the increasingly slack season in transatlantic liner travel, passenger ships would take their turns in drydock. For several weeks, while most of their normal staff went on well-earned leave, the liners would be invaded by small armies of shipyard crews—welders and electricians, painters and upholsterers. To meet rigid deadlines for delivery, there might be round-the-clock shifts and outdoor work in freezing temperatures. The ships, such as the* United States, *which went to the Newport News Shipyards in Virginia for a month or so each winter, would reappear in pristine, glowing form. A season of trans-ocean relays would then begin. (United States Lines.)*

Below *Dispensing smoke and soot effectively from the stacks of ocean liners has always been a matter of considerable concern. The early three-and four-stackers tended to have very tall, slender funnels that were practical in disposing of huge quantities of black coal smoke as well as hot, often fiery cinders. In the twenties and thirties there was a design trend toward low, squat stacks. Giving ships a sleek, racy appearance, they also showered layers of black and brown flakes on passengers resting in after-deck chairs. Many ships had their funnels raised in height. In the latter-day generation of the Atlantic liners, in the fifties and sixties, one of the most effective set of funnels was aboard the French flagship* France. *Her two large red and black stacks included sombrero-hat-like wings that, with help of special blowers, actually sent the smoke off to the sides of the ship rather than aft. So successful and noticeable were these stacks, that the French thoughtfully produced replicas that could be used as ashtrays.* (French Line.)

Bottom *When the Italians commissioned their largest and last set of post-war liners, the twin sisters* Michelangelo *and* Raffaello *of 1965, they used a most interesting funnel device. Positioned farther aft than most other twin-stackers, the funnels on these 45,000-ton ships were actually single, quite thin stovepipes. However, these were surrounded in a lattice-cage, very similar to the 'birdcage' masts found on early battleships, with large deflecting fins on top. Like the* France, *the two Italian sisters were easily recognizable by their smokestacks.* (Italian Line.)

Above left *In the autumn of 1958, as the first commercial jets began to fly the North Atlantic, the fate of the great liners was sealed. They fell, quite quickly, on hard, unprofitable times. In 1955, the Cunard Company had a fleet of nearly a dozen liners that carried a third of all passengers on the route to and from Europe. A decade later, they were losing millions and ready to abruptly retire as much as half of their diminished, demoded fleet. When the* Queen Mary *and* Queen Elizabeth *made their final crossings, in 1967 and 1968 respectively, each was showing an annual deficit of as much as £750,000 ($1,800,000). The ocean liner business had abruptly and rapidly changed, from transportation between distant continents to a new leisure series of cruiseships, randomly calling at exotic ports more for diversion.*

The France, *the last of the purposely built Atlantic superliners, finished her days under the Tricolour in September 1974. Even when filled to the very last upper berth in tourist class, she remained deep in debt. Her government sponsors saw little hope in her future and decided instead to subsidize the brand new Concorde. The world's longest liner was sent to a backwater berth at Le Havre, to await her fate. Five years later, after considerable rumour and an unsuccessful sale to an Arab millionaire, she went to the Norwegians, the Klosters Company of Oslo, who brilliantly—and boldly— decided to convert her into the world's largest cruiseship. In August 1979 she was towed to Bremerhaven to begin the transformation. (Hapag-Lloyd Shipyards.)*

Above right *At the Bremerhaven shipyards, owned by Hapag-Lloyd, a combination of the famed Hamburg American Line and North German Lloyd, the* France *underwent extensive cosmetic surgery. Hovered over by tall cranes, wrapped under acres of weather-resistant canvas and gradually stripped down to the original French steel, the* France *would be one of the few successful transformations of 'indoor' Atlantic liner to 'outdoor' tropic cruiseship. Most of the earlier ships went, quite sadly, to the scrapheap. Otherwise, the cruise industry, particularly in America, watched with high fascintion as the Norwegian Caribbean Lines, the Klosters' Miami-based cruise subsidiary, converted the* France *into the* Norway. *(Hapag-Lloyd Shipyards.)*

Below *Among other needs, the converted* Norway *required far more outdoor deck spaces. Two swimming pools amidst large lido decks were added. Rows and rows of deckchairs appeared, for those long hours in the Caribbean sun, where sheltered and enclosed spaces would have existed in her earlier French Line days. The enclosed promenade decks were converted to the largest shipboard carnival of shops ever—from perfumes and jewellery to designer clothes and even an ice cream shop. A large disco, complete with illuminated plexiglass floor, was added as was a Las Vegas style casino. The twin-level theatre, the largest ever to put to sea, was altered for cabaret-size, multi-media presentations.* (Hapag-Lloyd Shipyards.)

Bottom *Silent and deserted, the starboard promenade seems to echo of long gone Atlantic passengers, protected from the rigours of an often harsh North Atlantic as the ship once plied between Le Havre, Southampton and New York. Soon after this photo was taken, in the autumn of 1979, this area would be partly demolished, then rebuilt and reshaped, and finally transformed in a multi-coloured arcade of bars, shops and artificial flowers.* (Hapag-Lloyd Shipyards.)

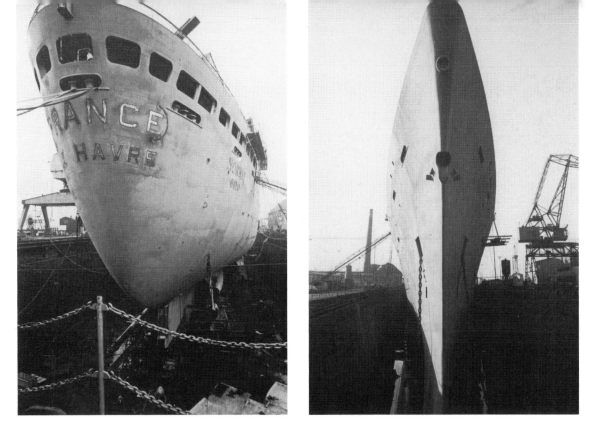

Above left *Operationally, the* France *had become an increasingly expensive ship to run. By the late seventies, with the enormous increases in the cost of fuel oil and labour, it would have been prohibitive without substantial change. As the* Norway, *she was sensibly reduced to a twin-screw liner, utilizing only one engine room and thereby cutting fuel oil costs. Built to run speeds as great as 30 kt, the new Norwegian flagship would be required, in the tranquil, sun-drenched waters of the Caribbean, to muster only as much as 16 kt. In fact, during the subsequent trials in the North Sea, even with a single engine room intact, she managed a most impressive 25 kt for a short stint. Other changes were arranged as well.* (Hapag-Lloyd Shipyards.)

Above right *The original 1,100 highly unionized staff members of the* France *were reduced to some 800 multi-national crew (with all Norwegian officers, however) as another efficient operating measure. On the other hand her capacity was increased, for supposed maximum revenue, from 1,944 to over 2,100. The latest navigational devices were added, two large tenders were positioned over the former forward hatches and televisions were added to every stateroom. The Atlantic 'ship of state' became the Caribbean 'state of the art' cruiseship. Completed in May 1980, she made a nostalgic crossing on the old run, from Oslo and Southampton to New York and then went on to her new home base at Miami. Thereafter she took up her intended role, weekly cruises to St Thomas, Nassau and a 'private' Out Island in the Bahamas. Four years later, in 1984, the £56.5 million ($130 million)* France/Norway *conversion was at last making a handsome profit. With a tonnage placed at over 70,200 tons, she is not only the largest liner afloat but one of the most successful and popular as well. Her Norwegian owners, so encouraged by her prospects, have talked of a 200,000-tonner, by far the largest passenger ship ever, capable of carrying over 4,000 passengers. If created, she would come into service in the late eighties.* (Hapag-Lloyd.)

Above far right *By the late seventies, all of the traditional transatlantic firms, with the exception of Cunard and their part time service between New York and Southampton with the* Queen Elizabeth 2, *had disappeared from the historic sealanes. In some cases the dissolution was dramatically fast; in others, the fleets gradually declined and dissipated over an extended time. Having one of the largest and last investments on the transatlantic run, the Italian Line remained until the very last possible moment, by which time their passenger ships were embarrassingly over-subsidized by a highly-criticized government in Rome. The disposal of their one time glorious fleet has been varied. The* Cristoforo Colombo, *sistership to the ill-fated* Andrea Doria, *was first rerouted to the South American trade, between Naples, Genoa, Rio and Buenos Aires, and then sent to the backwaters of the Orinoco River in Venezuela to serve as a hotel ship for the local steel workers. In 1980, she was towed out to Taiwan and subsequently scrapped. The* Augustus *and the* Giulio Cesare, *which served the New York run during peak summer seasons, were retired as well. The* Augustus *went to Far Eastern buyers, but only to be shifted from one lonely anchorage to another without further commercial purpose. The* Giulio Cesare *developed mechanical problems and was sold, without hesitation or thought of repairs, for scrapping.* (Port Authority of New York & New Jersey.)

Below *Among the saddest of all, however, were the three largest of these final Italian Line luxury ships. The* Leonardo da Vinci, *which ran the last crossing to Genoa and Naples in June 1976, was briefly detoured to the Bahamas cruising. Far less than successful, she was laid up at La Spezia, south of her former homeport of Genoa, but as the subject of persistent pressure from the Italian seamen's unions to reactivate her. Quite mysteriously, while empty and quietly anchored in the inner harbour, she burst into flames on 4 July 1980 and was destroyed totally. Her final fate was to capsize, a gaunt, scorched remnant—a dinosaur, in fact—of a recent, but bygone, era.*

The two newer sisterships, the Michelangelo *and* Raffaello, *were withdrawn in 1975 and then sold, two years later, to the Iranian government for use as military barracks ships. At present the* Michelangelo *is rusted and all but abandoned; the* Raffaello *is half-sunk following an Iraqi bombing. The fates of many transatlantic liners, happy ships in their day, have indeed been sad.* (Antonio Scrimali.)

Chapter 5

To all the seven seas

Soon after the close of the Second World War, the last great long-distance passenger ship services began to reopen. Apart from the more specialized and documented North Atlantic trade, these routes spanned the globe, on extended voyages that went out to South America, South Africa, the Middle East, Australia and the Orient. Aircraft would not be a serious threat for some time, in fact not until the late sixties and early seventies, and therefore these ships were assured of a steady flow of clientele. Most of them also carried cargo, not the express goods on the big transatlantic ships, but more varied products such as manufactured items, automobiles and then the localized cargoes such as gold, meat, wool, spice, tea and rubber. They were indeed the very last of their kind, mostly large combination passenger and cargo ships.

Britain's P&O Lines, known also as the P&O-Orient Lines from 1960 until 1966 after its merger with a longtime rival, the Orient Line, had the biggest and most important long-distance liner fleet in the post-war years. In fact, in 1960 P&O had the largest liner fleet anywhere, even surpassing the Cunard Company. An historic firm dating back to 1839 and which very much followed the creation of the British Empire, they were best known after the Second World War for the service out to Australia, to Fremantle, Melbourne and Sydney. The well-known Indian service, to Bombay, declined considerably after 1945, a result in part of India's changing political status. The Australian run was in a boom phase for over twenty years, with tourists, government officials, merchants, but mostly with outbound migrants. The specially promoted fare-assistance programme, allowing Britons to resettle 'down under' with passage fares as low as £10

($28), kept P&O liners filled to the very last upper bunk. One captain later recalled, 'We were so overcrowded, even in the mid sixties, that we had to place some of the migrants in first class cabins.'

In response to substantial war losses and then the foresight of profitable days ahead, the P&O and Orient lines embarked, soon after the war, on one of the biggest rebuilding programmes of all time. No less than seven liners, mostly in the 28,000-ton category, were created between 1948 and 1954. The Orient Line added a succession of three similar ships, the *Orcades* of 1948, the *Oronsay* of 1951 and the *Orsova* of 1954. Each was quite distinctive in grouping its funnel and mast (there was no mast whatsoever aboard the *Orsova*) high atop the bridge and closer to a midships position. They were most modern looking for their time. The P&O Lines, having had great success with their five Strath liners from the thirties, copied their basic design and arrangements and then used these with some refinements in the *Himalaya* of 1949, the *Chusan* of 1950 and finally in a pair of near-sisters, the *Arcadia* and *Iberia* of 1954.

The post-war P&O-Orient liners were merged with nine survivors from before the war, the *Orontes* and *Orion* of the Orient Line and the *Corfu*, *Carthage*, *Strathaird*, *Strathnaver*, *Strathmore*, *Stratheden* and *Canton* of P&O. They could easily provide weekly services out of London, via the Mediterranean, Suez and Ceylon, to Australia. In addition, there was a Far Eastern service, also from London, which also passed through the Suez Canal and then continued to South-east Asia and then northward along the Far East coast line.

Even in the mid fifties, as the North Atlantic

trade just began to rattle with the appearance of the aeroplane and then the jet, the P&O-Orient Australian route had a very promising future. It led the companies, P&O and Orient still being quite separate, to think of the two biggest and fastest liners ever built for a service other than transatlantic. The Orient liner came first, the 41,000-ton *Oriana*, the fastest ship ever to sail to Sydney, making the run out of Southampton via Suez in three weeks flat. It was said that she was the first British liner that could seriously substitute for one of the 28½-kt Cunard Queens on the Southampton-New York express run should the occasion arise. However, like the *United States* with the Blue Riband on the North Atlantic, the *Oriana*'s record was the last of any consequence. While no faster ships were built in fact, the appearance of aircraft within the next decade reduced her three-week passages to insignificance. P&O's new giant came several months later, the last in fact to come from the illustrious Harland & Wolff yards at Belfast, which had produced the likes of the *Titanic, Olympic* and dozens of other White Star passenger ships. Named *Canberra*, she reached 45,000 tons and could carry as many as 2,272 passengers (her capacity was even larger than the *Queen Elizabeth*, still the biggest liner afloat, with a total of 2,223 berths). Simultaneously, the P&O-Orient Lines, finally merged in preparation for the maiden sailings of these new giants, could advertise having the fastest as well as the largest liners on the Australian trade. Such distinctions would assure them, just as it had with the superlatives of 'biggest' and 'fastest' on the Atlantic, a steady flow of passengers. On her maiden departure from Southampton in June 1961, the *Canberra* left with 2,238 passengers onboard.

Architecturally and decoratively, P&O-Orient had shown steady improvement in their post-war liners. The public rooms grew larger and more contemporary in decor (especially aboard the *Oriana* and *Canberra*) and with such added features as lido bars, discos, conference rooms and even a multi-level theatre (on the *Oriana*). More cabins were fitted with private bathroom facilities, a consideration made more for the North American passengers that the Company hoped to attract by offering more voyages in the upper Pacific. The outdoor decks were larger than ever, with games areas, several pools and an abundance of comfortable sunchairs. By 1960, all of the post-war liners were given full air-conditioning throughout. Onboard entertainment, which was mostly passenger inspired and created, was later expanded to include an entertainments' officer and finally a full fledged cruise director, who produced an almost tiring schedule of all-day events, ranging from bingo to a squash competition to a lecture on flower arranging. Like the Atlantic companies, P&O began to recognize that the liners were more than just transport, they were floating hotels and resorts that must provide more and more recreation and amusement. Many of the older passengers, often in the first class quarters, travelled simply for travel's sake and while enjoying as much as a 100-day trip around the world, they very often remained aboard the ship while in port. A selection of P&O-Orient voyages in the winter of 1965–66 included:

Ship	Sailing	To
Chitral	9 November	Southampton, Port Said, Aden, Colombo, Penang, Port Swettenham, Singapore, Hong Kong, Yokohama, Shimizu, Kobe, Hong Kong, Singapore, Port Swettenham, Penang, Colombo, Aden, Port Said, Gibraltar and return to London; 74 days, fares from £478 ($1,338).
Orsova	14 November	London, Gibraltar, Naples, Port Said, Aden, Bombay, Penang, Singapore, Fremantle, Adelaide, Melbourne, Sydney, Melbourne, Adelaide, Fremantle, Colombo, Aden, Port Said, Malta, Naples, Ceuta, Flushing and return to London; 68 days, fares from £310 ($868) in tourist class.
Oriana	5 December	Southampton, Gibraltar, Naples, Port Said, Aden, Colombo, Fremantle, Melbourne, Sydney, Melbourne, Fremantle, Colombo, Aden, Port Said, Naples, Gibraltar and return to Southampton; 50 days, fares from £310 ($868) in tourist class.
Orcades	1 January	London, Flushing, Port Said, Aden, Colombo,

Ship	Sailing	To	Ship	Sailing	To
		Fremantle, Adelaide, Melbourne, Wellington, Sydney, Brisbane, Hong Kong, Singapore, Bombay, Aden, Port Said, Naples, Lisbon, and return to London; 75 days, fares from £364 ($1,019) in tourist class.			Said, Naples, Marseilles, Gibraltar and return to London; 97 days, fares from £434 ($1,215) in tourist class.
Cathay	8 January	Southampton, Port Said, Aden, Colombo, Penang, Port Swettenham, Singapore, Hong Kong, Singapore, Port Swettenham, Penang, Colombo, Aden, Port Said, Gibraltar and return to London; 74 days, fares from £506 ($1,417) in first class.	*Oriana*	8 February	Southampton, Gibraltar, Naples, Port Said, Aden, Colombo, Fremantle, Melbourne, Sydney, Auckland, Suva, Honolulu, Vancouver, San Francisco, Los Angeles, Honolulu, Yokohama, Kobe, Hong Kong, Singapore, Colombo, Aden, Port Said, Naples, Villefranche, Gibraltar and return to Southampton; 84 days, fares from £604 ($1,691) in tourist class.
Iberia	27 January	London, Gibraltar, Naples, Port Said, Aden, Bombay, Singapore, Fremantle, Adelaide, Melbourne, Sydney, Melbourne, Adelaide, Fremantle, Colombo, Bombay, Aden, Port Said, Naples, Marseilles, Gibraltar and return to London; 69 days, fares from £360 ($1,008) in tourist class.			
Chitral	6 February	London, Port Said, Aden, Colombo, Penang, Port Swettenham, Singapore, Hong Kong, Yokohama, Shimizu, Kobe, Hong Kong, Singapore, Port Swettenham, Penang, Colombo, Aden, Port Said, Gibraltar and return to London; 74 days, fares from £478 ($1,338) in first class.			
Orsova	8 February	London, Bermuda, Miami, Nassau, Panama, Acapulco, Los Angeles, San Francisco, Vancouver, Honolulu, Suva, Auckland, Sydney (21 days ashore), Melbourne, Adelaide, Fremantle, Colombo, Bombay, Aden, Port			

The P&O passenger fleet was first affected by aircraft competition in the late sixties. Responding to this first challenge, one company captain recalled, 'We sent our liners on longer and more diverse sailings, roaming the world looking for passengers to fill our increasingly empty berths.' Shortly thereafter there were other problems as well; container ships took the passenger ship cargoes, then inexpensive air charter flights went east of the Suez and lured away the few remaining passengers and finally, for the older, immediate post-war liners, new regulations came into effect that would have forced costly refits for liners nearing the age of 25. It became painfully obvious. Like so many others, especially in the early seventies, the P&O-Orient liners—like a parade of elephants—sailed off to the boneyards of the Far East. Between 1972 and 1976, the company retired the *Iberia, Orcades, Chusan, Himalaya, Orsova* and *Oronsay*. That vast global network of passenger ship services, including the many companies beyond P&O, was coming to an abrupt ending. In the years ahead, it would be far more difficult to sail out to South Africa or Australia or Japan.

In addition to P&O's dominant position on the Australia-New Zealand trades, a number of other firms had important interests there as well. Britain's Shaw Savill Line, primarily with their *Southern Cross*, the first liner to mount her engines and therefore her funnel aft, and her near-sister *Northern Star*, worked a 76-day around-the-world service that included calls at Fremantle, Melbourne, Sydney and Wellington. Another British firm, the New Zealand Shipping Company, ran several very large combination passenger-cargo ships out from London to Auckland and Wellington, but using the Panama route in both directions. Such ships also derived considerable incomes from the lucrative meat and wool trades. The Italians and Greeks also invested strongly, especially in view of the booming outward migrant trade. Companies such as the Lauro, Sitmar, Cogedar and Chandris Lines took second-hand ships, rebuilt them and in the process usually doubled their capacities, often with six- and eight-berth rooms. Homebound, they relied on discontented migrants and budget tourists bound for a holiday in Europe or Britain. The last Australian government migrant contract for sea travel was, in fact, given not to Britain's P&O but to the Greek Chandris Lines. Additionally, the Lloyd Triestino of Italy and the Messageries Maritimes of France also ran passenger ships to Australian ports.

Second to P&O only in the size of their fleet, Britain's Union-Castle Line ran as many as eight mail liners on the express route from Southampton to the South African Cape, to such ports as Capetown, Port Elizabeth, East London and Durban. It was considered the world's most precise service, sailing from the Southampton Docks every Thursday at the stroke of four in the afternoon, and then reaching Capetown two weeks later. The mails as well as special cargoes were delivered on time, based upon schedules that were issued as much as two years in advance. The 'Cape Mail Express' fleet in 1960 numbered eight major liners, the smallest of which was 20,000 tons. They were designed with long, flattish profiles and wide, low-standing funnels. Their hulls were painted in a unique lavender. Sailing in steady rotation, the group consisted of the *Carnarvon Castle*, *Winchester Castle*, *Athlone Castle*, *Stirling Castle*, *Capetown Castle*, *Pretoria Castle*, *Edinburgh Castle* and the *Pendennis Castle*. Shortly afterward, as the first phase of reduction, the service would be reduced to five mail liners, including the brand new *Windsor Castle* and *Transvaal Castle*, and two fast freighters. Within a decade, by the mid seventies, it was left to only two passenger ships before final termination. Since all of these ships had very large cargo capacities, a fatal blow was the appearance of giant, very fast container ships on the South African run. The story again repeated itself; lost cargo and dwindling passenger figures that resulted in increasing unprofitability. The

last Castle liners finished their voyages in the autumn of 1977.

Prompted by Britain's large colonial holdings in Africa, especially along the East Coast, Union-Castle also ran a nine-week Round Africa service out of London. Alternating between Suez or South Atlantic outward and then reversing for the homeward trip, the ports of call included Mombasa, Tanga, Dar-es-Salaam, Zanzibar and Walvis Bay. A rival on the same trade, but limited only to the East Coast ports, was the British India Line. The West African route was also worked by the Elder Dempster Line. To the southern and eastern coasts, the enormous Ellerman Group ran four combination liners, carrying substantial quantities of freight and 107 passengers in very de luxe, yacht-like quarters. The Europeans had passenger ship interests to Africa as well; the Holland-Africa Line to South Africa, the Belgian Line to the colonial Congo, Messageries Maritimes to East Africa and Madagascar, the Compagnie Paquet to West Africa, Portugal's Companhia Colonial and Companhia Nacional to outposts in Angola and Mozambique and even Italy's Lloyd Triestino, which plied the East African trade, reminiscent of their pre-war military campaigns.

As the African trades had their speciality cargoes even for passenger ships, such as gold, fruits and spices, the Latin American passenger routes were largely dependent on the meats coming out of the Argentine. There was also coffee, furs and fruits. Britain's Royal Mail and Blue Star lines worked the East Coast trade to Rio, Santos, Montevideo and then a lengthy turnaround (for cargo handling) at Buenos Aires. The Booth Line, based at Liverpool, plied a more exotic trade; along the Amazon as far as Manaus. The Pacific Steam Navigation Company used the alternate coast, to Ecuador, Peru and Chile, via Panama. Especially for the important outbound migrant trade, a large number of passenger ships, most of them rebuilt from earlier lives, sailed out of the Mediterranean. Italy's Costa Line, which first entered passenger shipping in 1948, later had the largest fleet, which included the brand new 30,000-ton *Eugenio C* of 1966. There was also the Italian Line (running an alternate service to its more luxurious trade to New York), Spain's Ybarra Line and France's Compagnie Sud-Atlantique. Even the Argentines themselves became involved, running several combination liners to New York and London as well as high-capacity emigrant ships out of Hamburg, Amsterdam, Genoa, Naples and Lisbon. The Portuguese had a 21,000-tonner, the *Vera Cruz*, on the run to Brazilian ports. Out of America, although more cruise-like in nature in their later years, the *Santa* ships of the Grace Line and the *Argentina* and *Brasil* of Moore-McCormack traded to southern ports.

The Caribbean area was served by such ships as the passenger-carrying 'banana boats' of Elders & Fyffes, combination ships from the Royal Netherlands Steamship Company and converted emigrant types from the Italian Siosa Lines and the Spanish Line. There were also the colonial links to Martinique and Guadeloupe worked by two very fine French liners, the 20,000-ton near-sisters *Antilles* and *Flandre*.

On the often steamy passages east of the Suez, to Middle and Far Eastern ports, were the Anchor Line to India, the Bibby Line to Burma and the Blue Funnel, Lloyd Triestino, Hamburg American, North German Lloyd and P&O ships to such ports as Hong Kong, Kobe and Yokohama. Across the Pacific, Japan's Mitsui-OSK Lines ran an extensive migrant trade through Panama to the East Coast of South America. The American President Lines traded to the Orient, to Japan, Hong Kong and the Philippines. Another American firm, the Matson Line, provided a link to the Hawaiian islands as well as deep into the South Pacific, to Polynesia, New Zealand and Australia.

There were, of course, the short-distance passenger ship trades, such as Blue Funnel Line's long established link between Singapore and western Australia, the Burns Philp Line out of Sydney to the South Sea islands and British India's complex of operations from Bombay along the Persian Gulf and then further afield to the Seychelles and East Africa, from Calcutta to South-east Asia and to Far Eastern ports as far north as Japan. Aircraft dealt the final blow to these localized services as well, even securing the once guaranteed travellers in third and deck classes.

Perhaps the most extensive passenger network, aside from the worldwide operations of P&O-Orient, was Holland's Royal Interocean Lines. While they never visited home waters, their major ships traded between three continents, from the East Coast of South America to South and East Africa and then to South-east Asia and finally the Far East. In addition, they ran a triangular service from Australia to Hong Kong and Japan, and then homeward via the Pacific islands, as well as a link between India and Australia.

The intensity of diverse passenger ship sailings in these final pre-aircraft years is exemplified in this sailing list from the port of Southampton for November 1962:

Ship	Company	From/to
Thursday 1 November		
Queen Elizabeth	Cunard	to New York
Capetown Castle	Union-Castle	to Capetown
Castel Felice	Stimar	from Sydney
Friday 2 November		
France	French Line	to New York
Athlone Castle	Union-Castle	from Capetown
Saturday 3 November		
Oranje	Nederland Line	from Wellington
Ryndam	Holland-America	from Montreal
Breconshire	Glen Line	to Yokohama
Venus	Bergen Line	from Madeira
Sunday 4 November		
Antilles	French Line	from Trinidad
Fairsea	Sitmar	from Auckland
Prinses Irene	Oranje	to Toronto
Monday 5 November		
Queen Mary	Cunard	from New York
Berlin	North German	to New York
Castel Felice	Sitmar	to Sydney
Tuesday 6 November		
	No calls	
Wednesday 7 November		
United States	US Lines	from New York
Thursday 8 November		
Queen Mary	Cunard	to New York
Pendennis Castle	Union-Castle	to Capetown
Flandre	French Line	from New York
Friday 9 November		
Nieuw Amsterdam	Holland-America	from New York
Bremen	North German Lloyd	from New York
Edinburgh Castle	Union-Castle	from Capetown
Maasdam	Holland-America	from New York
Ryndham	Holland-America	to Montreal
Saturday 10 November		
United States	US Lines	to New York
Antilles	French Line	to Trinidad
Randfontein	Holland-Africa Line	from Capetown
Jagersfontein	Holland-Africa Line	to Capetown

Ship	Company	From/to
Willemstad	Royal Netherlands	to Georgetown
Sunday 11 November		
Andes	Royal Mail	Mediterranean cruise
Carinthia	Cunard	from Montreal
Faìrsea	Sitmar	to Sydney
Frankfurt	Hamburg-America	to Yokohama
Monday 12 November		
Andes	Royal Mail	to West Indies cruise
Tuesday 13 November		
Queen Elizabeth	Cunard	from New York
France	French Line	from New York
Begona	Spanish Line	from Trinidad
Wednesday 14 November		
Bremen	North German Lloyd	to New York
Carinthia	Cunard	to Montreal
Maasdam	Holland-America	to New York
Begona	Spanish Line	to Kingston
Thursday 15 November		
Athlone Castle	Union-Castle	to Capetown
Oranje	Nederland Line	to Sydney
Friday 16 November		
Queen Elizabeth	Cunard	to New York
France	French Line	to New York
Rotterdam	Holland-America	from New York
America	US Lines	from New York
Stirling Castle	Union-Castle	from Capetown
Colombie	French Line	from Trinidad
Prins der Nederlanden	Royal Netherlands	to Kingston
Saturday 17 November		
Oxfordshire	Bibby	from Hong Kong
Sunday 18 November		
Chitral	P&O-Orient	to Yokohama
Prinses Margriet	Oranje	to Montreal
Monday 19 November		
No calls		
Tuesday 20 November		
Queen Mary	Cunard	from New York
America	US Lines	to New York
Brittany	Chandris	from Sydney
Wednesday 21 November		
Colombie	French Line	to Trinidad

Ship	Company	From/to
Thursday 22 November		
Edinburgh Castle	Union-Castle	to Capetown
Brittany	Chandris	to Sydney
Hannover	Hamburg-America	to Yokohama
Friday 23 November		
Queen Mary	Cunard	to New York
Windsor Castle	Union-Castle	from Capetown
Nieuw Amsterdam	Holland-America	to New York
Saturday 24 November		
Schwabenstein	North German Lloyd	from Yokohama
Sunday 25 November		
Southern Cross	Shaw Savill	from Auckland
Monday 26 November		
Caronia	Cunard	Mediterranean cruise
Batory	Gdynia America	to Quebec City
Ascania	Grimaldi-Siosa	to Kingston
Tuesday 27 November		
No calls		
Wednesday 28 November		
Queen Elizabeth	Cunard	from New York
France	French Line	from New York
Bremen	North German Lloyd	from New York
Ryndam	Holland-America	from Montreal
Thursday 29 November		
Rotterdam	Holland-America	to New York
Stirling Castle	Union-Castle	to Capetown
Friday 30 November		
France	French Line	to New York
Pretoria Castle	Union-Castle	from Capetown

Within a decade, by the early seventies, most of these services had ceased. Aircraft competition, increased labour and fuel costs, the transition to container cargo shipping and the general maturity of many ships combined to spell their ends. Some of the shipowners themselves disbanded and discontinued trading as well. In 1973, marine fuel oil charges jumped dramatically from £14 ($35) to £39 ($95) a ton and consequently prompted the greatest procession of ships to the breakers' yards in all of ocean liner history. A listing for a seven-year period, between 1970–77, included:

Ship/owner or flag	Tonnage	Date	Scrapyard
Margarita (1944, Greek) ex-*Waterman* (Dutch)	9,900	February 1970	Japan
Sun (1946, American) ex-*Santa Sofia* (Grace Line)	8,300	February 1970	Taiwan
Julia (1946, American) ex-*Santa Cecilia* (Grace Line)	8,300	April 1970	Taiwan
King Abdelaziz (1946, Saudi Arabian) ex-*Flaminia* (Cogedar Line)	8,700	April 1970	Taiwan
Rio Jachal (1951, Argentine)	11,300	April 1970	Argentina
Wanganella (1932, ex-Australian)	9,800	May 1970	Taiwan
Sofia (1946, American) ex-*Santa Isabel* (Grace Line)	8,300	July 1970	Taiwan
Bled (1945, Yugoslav)	7,700	July 1970	Italy
Marianna IV (1944, Greek) ex-*Groote Beer* (Dutch)	9,900	July 1970	Greece
Cosmos Mariner (1946, American) ex-*Santa Sofia* (Grace Line)	8,300	August 1970	Taiwan
Castel Felice (1930, Sitmar Line) ex-*Kenya* (British India)	10,900	October 1970	Taiwan
Citta di Tunisi (1930, Tirrenia)	5,400	November 1970	Italy
Santa Anna (1924, Panamanian) ex-*Contessa* (Standard Fruit)	5,300	November 1970	Italy
Glenearn (1938, Glen Line)	8,800	November 1970	Taiwan
Bovec (1945, Yugoslav)	7,700	December 1970	China
George Anson (1948, Dominion) ex-*Newfoundland* (Furness Withy)	7,700	February 1971	Taiwan
Glengarry (1939, Glen Line)	9,300	February 1971	Taiwan
Francis Drake (1947, Dominion) ex-*Nova Scotia* (Furness Withy)	7,700	March 1971	Taiwan
Caledonia (1948, Anchor Line)	11,200	April 1971	West Germany
Andes (1939, Royal Mail Lines)	25,800	April 1971	Belgium
Batory (1936, Polish Ocean Lines)	14,200	May 1971	Hong Kong
Kampala (1947, British India)	10,300	July 1971	Taiwan
Safina-e-Siahat (1951, Pakistani) ex-*Général Leclerc* (French)	9,400	September 1971	Pakistan
Anna C (1929, Costa Line) ex-*Southern Prince* (Furness)	12,000	December 1971	Italy
Golfito (1949, Elders & Fyffes)	8,300	December 1971	Scotland
Kuala Lumpur (1936, China Navigation) ex-*Dilwara* (P&O)	12,500	December 1971	Taiwan
Bothinj (1946, Yugoslav)	7,700	January 1972	Yugoslavia
Del Mar (1946, Delta Line)	10,000	February 1972	Taiwan
Del Norte (1946, Delta Line)	10,000	February 1972	Taiwan
Del Sud (1946, Delta Line)	10,000	February 1972	Taiwan
Ixion (1951, Blue Funnel Line)	9,700	March 1972	Spain
Jason (1950, Blue Funnel Line)	9,700	May 1972	Taiwan
Ceramic (1948, Shaw Savill Line)	15,000	June 1972	Belgium
Hector (1950, Blue Funnel Line)	9,700	July 1972	Taiwan
Helenus (1950, Blue Funnel Line)	9,700	July 1972	Taiwan
Peleus (1949, Blue Funnel Line)	9,700	July 1972	Taiwan
State of Bombay (1948, Indian)	8,500	August 1972	India
Iberia (1954, P&O)	29,700	September 1972	Taiwan
Armelle (1945, Somali) ex-*Hrvatska* (Yugoslav)	7,900	September 1972	Spain
Sirdhana (1947, British India)	8,600	September 1972	Taiwan

Ship/owner or flag	Tonnage	Date	Scrapyard
Pyrrhus (1949, Blue Funnel Line)	9,600	September 1972	Taiwan
Uruguay Star (1948, Blue Star)	10,500	September 1972	Taiwan
Argentina Star (1947, Blue Star)	10,500	September 1972	Taiwan
Brasil Star (1947, Blue Star)	10,500	September 1972	Taiwan
Moçambique (1949, Cia Nacional)	12,900	October 1972	Taiwan
Carvalho Araujo (1930, Portuguese)	4,500	November 1972	Portugal
Argentina (1949, Argentine)	12,400	January 1973	Argentina
ex-*Presidente Perón* (Argentine)			
Australasia (1950, Austasia Line)	10,800	January 1973	Taiwan
ex-*Iberia Star* (Blue Star)			
ex-*Anselm* (Booth Line)			
ex-*Thysville* (Belgian Line)			
ex-*Baudouinville* (Belgian Line)			
Perseus (1949, Blue Funnel Line)	9,700	January 1973	Taiwan
Uruguay (1949, Argentine)	12,600	January 1973	Argentina
ex-*Eva Perón* (Argentine)			
Orcades (1948, P&O)	28,400	February 1973	Taiwan
Montserrat (1945, Spanish Line)	9,000	March 1973	Spain
ex-*Castel Verde* (Sitmar)			
Vanmint (1950, Panamanian)	8,300	March 1973	Taiwan
ex-*America Maru* (Mitsui Line)			
Albertville (1950, Belgian Line)	10,500	April 1973	Taiwan
Camito (1956, Elders & Fyffes)	8,500	April 1973	Taiwan
Covadonga (1953, Spanish Line)	10,200	April 1973	Spain
Guadalupe (1953, Spanish Line)	10,200	April 1973	Spain
Vera Cruz (1952, Cia Colonial)	21,700	April 1973	Taiwan
Giulio Cesare (1951, Italian Line)	27,000	May 1973	Italy
State of Maine (1939, American)	9,900	May 1973	USA
ex-*Ancon* (Panama Line)			
Chusan (1950, P&O)	24,300	June 1973	Taiwan
Ville de Marseille (1951, French)	9,500	June 1973	Spain
Alfredo da Silva (1950, Portuguese)	3,300	June 1973	Spain
Floriana (1952, Greek)	7,600	June 1973	Spain
ex-*El Djezair* (Cie Mixte)			
Santa Maria (1953, Cia Colonial)	20,900	July 1973	Taiwan
Patria (1948, Cia Colonial)	13,100	August 1973	Taiwan
Manuel Alfredo (1954, Portuguese)	3,400	September 1973	Spain
State of Madras (1948, Indian)	8,600	September 1973	India
ex-*Jalajawahar* (Scindia line)			
Cynthia (1929, Hellenic Mediterranean)	4,600	October 1973	Italy
ex-*Britannia* (Swedish Lloyd)			
Petr Velikiy (1939, Soviet)	6,200	November 1973	Spain
Oriental Rio (1951, Tung Group)	17,700	December 1973	Taiwan
ex-*Ruahine* (New Zealand Shipping)			
Homeric (1931, Home Lines)	18,500	January 1974	Taiwan
ex-*Mariposa* (Matson Lines)			
Isla de Cabrera (1948, Spanish)	6,600	February 1974	Spain
ex-*Satrustegui* (Spanish Line)			
Wicklow (1950, Panamanian)	8,600	February 1974	China
ex-*Eastern Queen* (Dominion)			
Oriental Jade (1944, Tung Group)	9,600	February 1974	Taiwan
ex-*Excalibur* (American Export)			
Orsova (1954, P&O)	29,000	February 1974	Taiwan
Arosa Sun (1930, Dutch)	17,000	March 1974	Spain
ex-*Félix Roussel* (French)			

Ship/owner or flag	Tonnage	Date	Scrapyard
Massalia (1937, Hellenic Mediterranean) ex-*Bretagne* (Fred Olsen Line)	3,200	March 1974	Greece
Oriental Pearl (1944, Tung Group) ex-*Exeter* (American Export)	9,600	March 1974	Taiwan
Delphi (1952, Efthymiadis Lines) ex-*Ferdinand de Lesseps* (French)	10,800	March 1974	Spain
Isthmia (1929, Hellenic Mediterranean) ex-*Suecia* (Swedish Lloyd)	4,600	March 1974	Turkey
Kairouan (1950, Cie Mixte)	8,600	March 1974	Spain
Maori (1953, Union Line)	8,300	March 1974	Taiwan
Miriam B (1938, Saudi Lines) ex-*Oranjestad* (Royal Netherlands)	5,000	March 1974	Taiwan
Nieuw Amsterdam (1938, Holland-America)	36,700	March 1974	Taiwan
Imperio (1948, Cia Colonial)	13,100	March 1974	Taiwan
Mediterranean Dolphin (1954, Greek) ex-*City of Durban* (Ellerman)	13,200	March 1974	Taiwan
Fantasia (1935, Chandris Cruises) ex-*Duke of York* (British Rail)	4,500	March 1974	Spain
Agamemnon (1953, Dorian Cruises)	5,500	May 1974	Spain
Oriental President (1948, Tung Group) ex-*President Cleveland* (American President)	15,400	June 1974	Taiwan
Caribia (1928, Siosa Lines) ex-*Vulcania* (Italian Line)	24,400	July 1974	Taiwan (sank at approaches to dockyard)
P. E. Lumumba (1950, Cie Zaire) ex-*Léopoldville* (Belgian Line)	10,500	August 1974	Brazil
Atlantica (1931, Typaldos Lines) ex-*Colombie* (French Line)	13,800	August 1974	Spain
Caribia 2 (1944, Greek) ex-*Roma* (Lauro Line) ex-*Sydney* (Lauro Line)	14,900	August 1974	Italy
Himalaya (1949, P&O)	28,000	November 1974	Taiwan
Begona (1945, Spanish Line) ex-*Castel Bianco* (Sitmar)	10,100	December 1974	Spain
Nevasa (1956, British India)	20,100	March 1975	Taiwan
Taiphooshan (1948, Shun Cheong) ex-*Apapa* (Elder Dempster)	11,600	March 1975	Taiwan
Gruzia (1939, Soviet) ex-*Sobieski* (Gdynia America)	11,000	April 1975	Italy
President Hayes (1940, American)	10,200	May 1975	USA
Ocean Monarch (1957, Shaw Savill) ex-*Empress of England* (Canadian Pacific)	25,900	July 1975	Taiwan
Libertad (1950, Argentine) ex-*17 De Octubre* (Argentine)	12,600	July 1975	Argentina
Reina del Mar (1956, Union Castle)	20,700	July 1975	Taiwan
Stevens (1944, American) ex-*Exochorda* (American Export)	9,600	August 1975	USA
Oronsay (1951, P&O)	28,100	October 1975	Taiwan
S. A. Oranje (1948, Safmarine) ex-*Pretoria Castle* (Union Castle)	27,500	November 1975	Taiwan
Northern Star (1961, Shaw Savill)	23,900	December 1975	Taiwan
Nessebar (1946, Bulgarian) ex-*Ville de Bordeaux* (French Line) ex-*Saga* (Swedish Lloyd)	6,500	December 1975	Yugoslavia

Ship/owner or flag	Tonnage	Date	Scrapyard
Chitral (1956, P&O) ex-*Jadotville* (Belgian Line)	13,800	December 1975	Taiwan
Oriental Carnaval (1949, Tung Group) ex-*Rangitoto* (New Zealand Shipping)	19,600	February 1976	Taiwan
Highland Queen (1930, Greek) ex-*Hermes* (Epirotiki Lines) ex-*Princess Elizabeth* (Canadian Pacific)	5,200	March 1976	Belgium
Oriental Esmeralda (1949, Tung Group) ex-*Rangitane* (New Zealand Shipping)	19,500	April 1976	Taiwan
Edinburgh Castle (1948, Union Castle)	27,400	June 1976	Taiwan
Safina-e-Hujjaj (1935, Pakistani) ex-*Empire Fowey* (P&O) ex-*Potsdam* (North German Lloyd)	19,100	October 1976	Pakistan
Nippon Maru (1958, Mitsui Lines) ex-*Argentina Maru* (Mitsui Lines)	10,700	December 1976	Taiwan
State of Haryana (1950, Indian) ex-*Santhia* (British India)	8,900	January 1977	India
Rio Tunuyan (1951, Argentine) ex-*Evita* (Argentine)	11,400	February 1977	Argentina
Carina (1930, Chandris Cruises) ex-*Princess Hélène* (Canadian Pacific)	3,800	March 1977	Greece
Malaysia Raya (1953, Compania Abeto) ex-*Empress Abeto* (Compania Abeto) ex-*Laos* (Messageries Maritimes)	13,500	April 1977	Taiwan
Queen Frederica (1927, Chandris) ex-*Atlantic* (Home Lines) ex-*Matsonia* (Matson Lines) ex-*Malolo* (Matson Lines)	16,400	May 1977	Greece
Seven Seas (1940, Europe-Canada Line)	12,500	May 1977	Belgium
Climax Opal (1952, Singapore) ex-*Monte Ulia* (Aznar Line)	10,100	June 1977	Spain
Verdi (1951, Italian Line) ex-*Oceania* (Lloyd Triestino)	13,200	June 1977	Italy
Mozaffari (1948, Mogul Line)	7,000	August 1977	India
Knossos (1953, Efthymiadis Lines) ex-*La Bourdonnais* (Messageries Maritimes)	10,800	August 1977	Greece
Kim Hock (1951, Singapore) ex-*India* (Cia Nacional)	7,600	August 1977	Taiwan
Rossini (1951, Italian Line) ex-*Neptunia* (Lloyd Triestino)	13,200	September 1977	Italy

At the time of writing, in 1985, there are just about two passenger services still advertised that reflect these earlier overseas trades. The Belgians run a pair of 71-passenger combination ships, the *Fabiolaville* and the *Kananga* (the latter flies the flag of Zaïre), on the remains of the old colonial Congo trade from Antwerp via Tenerife, Dakar and Abidjan. The second service, while using the small *St Helena*, a 2,500-tonner formerly on the Alaska intercoastal trade, also trades between Britain and the South Atlantic, between Avonmouth, Tenerife, St Vincent, St Helena, Ascension and Capetown. She carries a scant 88 passengers.

The once numerous liner trades that spanned the globe are now gone and those busy routes—trans-Suez, transpacific and tropic—are now as desolate as the North Atlantic.

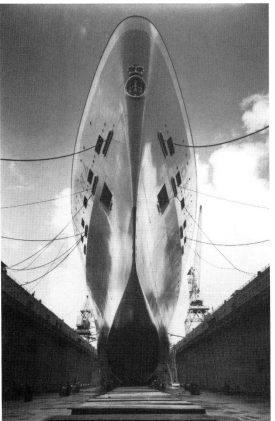

Above *Last of the grand era for the Australian liners, the 41,000-ton Oriana of Britain's Orient Line glides down the slipway of the Barrow-in-Furness yard of Vickers-Armstrong for the first time, in November 1959. Huge chains are attached to temporary brackets placed along her hull and which will serve as a brake to slow the ship's launching speed soon after she is waterborne. Workers at the shipyard, proud of their accomplishment thus far, doff their caps in wishing her safe travels. Princess Alexandra of Kent, a cousin to Queen Elizabeth, had given the ship a royal christening. (P&O Group.)*

Left *Twelve months after launching, the Oriana was delivered and handed over to her owners in an official ceremony. Those final months at the yard had been busy to meet the tightly scheduled delivery date. Masts and funnels had to be put in place, carpets laid, furniture brought aboard and arranged, artwork installed, specialized equipment added and all while thousands of gallons of paint covered the entire ship for the first time. Just prior to her record breaking maiden voyage out from Southampton to Fremantle, Melbourne and Sydney via Suez, the Oriana was dry docked at Falmouth for last-minute alterations and fine tuning. The bulbous bow of the 804 ft long liner is clearly visible in this artistic photograph. (P&O Group.)*

Right *Almost simultaneously, at the Harland & Wolff yards at Belfast, the P&O Lines were preparing for their new flagship, the 45,700-ton* Canberra, *the largest liner yet built for a service other than the North Atlantic. She would appear for the first time some six months after the* Oriana, *in June 1961. She too would run on the Australian route, but would also make extended voyages into the Pacific, on to North America and, on occasion, go completely around the globe. Like the* Oriana, *she was built for the final era of seagoing migrant and tourist transport to areas east of the Suez. For about a decade, both ships enjoyed considerable success and profit.* (P&O Group.)

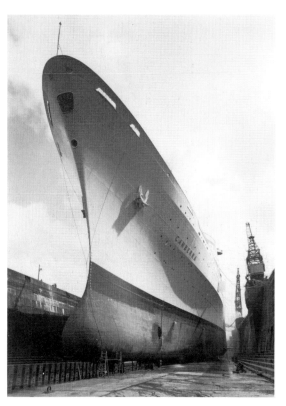

Below *Amidst a web of scaffolding, the outer starboard side propellor of the mighty* Canberra, *can be seen in this view taken at the King George V Graving Dock at Southampton. As a matter of routine, both the* Canberra *and* Oriana *spent 14-21 days each year undergoing annual overhaul, repairs and inspections.* (Southern Newspapers Limited.)

Below left *In the early years of her P&O liner service, the* Canberra *was often booked to her full capacity of 2,272 passengers—556 in first class and 1,716 in tourist. Looked after by over 800 crew members, the liner sailed on an often changing pattern of voyages. Passages could be booked for as many as 140 days or as little as an overnight run. On one of her longer trips, the* Canberra *set sail from Southampton for Gibraltar, Naples, Piraeus and Port Said, then passed through the Suez Canal and headed for Colombo, Fremantle, Melbourne, Sydney and Auckland. From there, she proceeded to Suva, Honolulu, Vancouver, San Francisco and Los Angeles. Homeward bound, she called at Acapulco, Cristobal, Kingston, Port Everglades, Nassau and Bermuda, before reaching Southampton over 110 days later. Minimum tourist class fares for the full voyage began, in the late sixties, at £800 ($1,920). (P&O Group.)*

Below right *The post-war P&O-Orient liners included the still popular 'Straths', the famed 'white ships' from the thirties. The* Strathnaver *and her sistership, the* Strathaird, *were the oldest of all, dating from 1931-32. Replaced in the early fifties by newer, faster tonnage, they were relegated to the low-fare emigrant trade, carrying over 1,200 passengers in all-tourist-class quarters, on the ever-booming trade between London, Gibraltar, Port Said, Aden, Ceylon, Fremantle, Melbourne and Sydney. Having been three-stackers until the end of the war, they were converted during their post-war refits to single-stackers, thereby resembling more closely their two surviving near-sisters, the* Strathmore *and* Stratheden. *Later, as the migrant trade began to slowly decline and then shift entirely to aircraft, the 'Straths' went their way. The two older ships were scrapped in the early sixties; the* Strathmore *and* Stratheden *finished out their days as Greek 'pilgrim ships' on Moslem trade before being scrapped in 1969. (P&O Group.)*

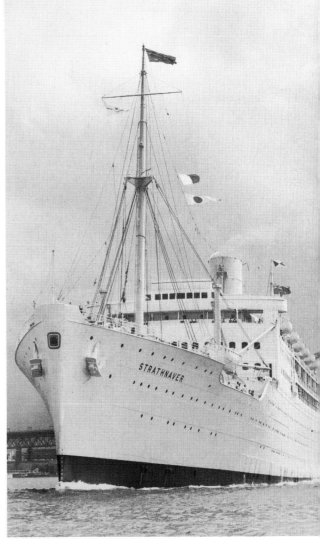

While the Canberra *was the largest liner of all on the Australian run, the* Oriana *was the slightly faster and secured the 'Golden Cockerel' for the swiftest passage ever between Southampton and Sydney, a flat 21 days. While built for different companies, the owners of these two ships sensibly merged their operations just before their maiden sailings as the P&O-Orient Lines. This unity gave them the largest deep-sea ocean liner fleet of all at the time, sixteen ships in all. While the* Canberra *used a design that placed her uptakes aft (instead of the customary midships funnel), therefore creating substantial passenger spaces in the centre of the ship, the* Oriana *was even less conventional. A single stack, placed on her very top deck, was her highest feature. Not even the radar mast forward of the bridge was equal in height. A second, funnel-like device—which was actually a ventilator—was positioned on a lower, aft deck. Consequently, the* Oriana *appeared to be a twin-stacker, but with one funnel 'up' and the other funnel 'down'. (P&O Group.)*

Left *The combined P&O-Orient Lines post-war liner rebuilding programme was one of the largest of all, totalling some 200,000 tons. The Orient Line began with the* Orcades *of 1948, followed by the* Oronsay *of 1951 and then the* Orsova *of 1954. P&O started with the* Himalaya *of 1949, then* Chusan *of 1950 and finished with a pair of near-sisters, the* Arcadia *and* Iberia *of 1954. Large ships, averaging some 28,000 tons and over 700 ft in length, they were designed with considerable open-air deck spaces, an essential ingredient for their steamy passages through the Suez Canal, Red Sea and Indian Ocean. By the late fifties, however, all of these liners were taken in hand for upgrading, which included the installation of complete air-conditioning. (P&O Group.)*

Below *Apart from London (or Southampton for the larger* Oriana *and* Canberra), *Sydney was the most important and frequently visited port on the P&O-Orient liner schedules. From that Australian port, the ships made their way on the customary route from England via the Suez (and later, after the Canal closed, via South Africa). They also spread out into other directions, especially beginning in the late fifties, to the Far East—to such ports as Singapore, Manila, Hong Kong, Kobe and Yokohama; to the North American West Coast—to Vancouver, San Francisco and Los Angeles; or on an alternate homeward run via the Panama Canal—to Cristobal, Kingston, Port Everglades, Nassau and Bermuda. In this view, the* Oronsay *is departing from Sydney on a triangular Pacific sailing, to Honolulu and then the American West Coast before crossing to the Far East and finally returning to Australia. From there she will return to London via Colombo, Bombay, Aden, Port Said, Naples, Marseilles and Gibraltar. (P&O Group.)*

Right *As the P&O-Orient Lines grew to a worldwide passenger ship operation, their large ships often began to appear in some of the world's smallest ports. In this scene, local youngsters at Pago Pago on American Samoa enjoy an afternoon with the mooring lines of the* Arcadia. *(P&O Group.)*

Below *To many travellers, one of the greatest lures to sailing with 'the P&O', as they were often termed, was the passage through the Suez Canal. Surrounded by hundreds upon hundreds of square miles of sand and near-desolation, the setting seemed to step off Kipling's pages. The big white P&O liners joined the customary convoys of ships, processions going southbound or later in the opposite direction. While temperatures often reached well over 100°F, the outer decks were lined with often sweltering, but mostly enchanted passengers. In the moodful scene below, the* Strathnaver's *bow is seen following in the wake of a small freighter. (P&O Group.)*

Left *The P&O-Orient liners were also well known for their cruise voyages, either as all-first-class or combination first-and-tourist-class ships. There were voyages such as six days in the* Himalaya *to Copenhagen and Amsterdam; thirteen days in the* Chusan *to Madeira, Teneriffe, Gibraltar and Lisbon; eighteen days in the* Iberia *to Corfu, Piraeus, Naples, Cannes and Barcelona; and thirty days in the* Oronsay *to Oporto, Teneriffe, Barbados, Antigua, St Thomas, San Juan, Nassau and Madeira. In this photograph, cruise passengers are disembarking from the* Oronsay *at Palma, in 1960. (P&O Group.)*

Below *When P&O-Orient expanded its passenger ship network to the North American West Coast, to Vancouver, San Francisco and Los Angeles, it was a considerable gamble. The company was unknown to most North Americans. The directors, however, saw the entire Pacific as the 'last frontier' of ocean travel. It could, so they thought, be developed similarly to the busy North Atlantic. It all took patience, however. Among the first of their ships to call there, the* Orion *put into San Francisco with a mere hundred passengers on board. Several years later, in 1960, there were as many as fifteen P&O sailings out of that same port. (Richard K. Morse Collection.)*

Right *P&O also developed a strong and very popular reputation for its cruises out of Sydney. Well known to Australians, many of which had emigrated on earlier voyages out from Britain, ships such as the* Himalaya *and* Arcadia *(shown arriving at Suva) were strong favourites. There were short trips, such as along the Great Barrier Reef, to Tasmania or across to New Zealand; two- and three-week runs to the South Pacific islands, to such ports as Noumean, Suva, Savu Savu, Pago Pago and Nuku'Alofa; and then the occasional longer cruises, for as much as six or seven weeks, to Singapore, Manila, Hong Kong, Keelung, Kobe, Yokohama and Guam. (P&O Group.)*

Left *The flagship of the Orient Line for some years, the* Orsova *was a noteworthy ship in passenger liner design annals. She was the first major ship to dispense with the conventional mast. Her single, large smokestack was the centre piece from which all necessary rigging was attached. An innovative element, it succeeded in giving the* Orsova *a special, readily identifiable appearance.* (P&O Group.)

Below *In addition to its large liner services, particularly out to Australia, P&O also ran a Far Eastern passenger run, using the 13,800-ton sisters* Cathay *and* Chitral *(shown in a night-time loading scene at Southampton). Carrying considerable freight and some 240 all-first-class passengers, they were routed from London, Rotterdam and Southampton to Port Said, Aden, Colombo, Penang, Port Swettenham, Singapore, Hong Kong, Yokohama and then a turnaround at Kobe. Their high-standard passenger accommodation, which included large staterooms, comfortable lounges and outdoor swimming pool, was very popular and, to many, resembled the intimacies of large yachts. In their cargo holds, these ships sailed outbound from Britain with manufacutred goods and then returned, especially in later years, with diverse quantities of the inexpensive mass produced goods so commonly associated with the East.* (P&O Group.)

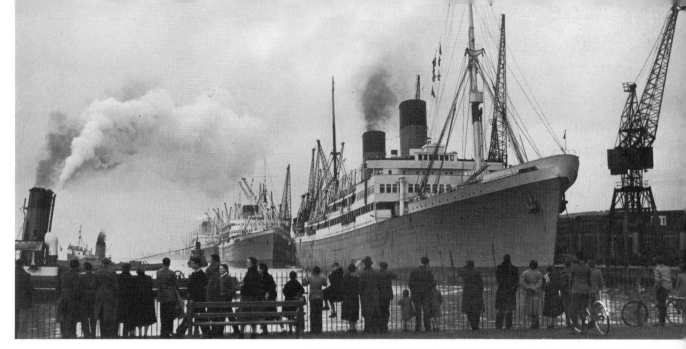

Above *Another British passenger ship company, the Union-Castle Line, had the best known name in the African trades. Most famous of all was their 'Cape Mail Express', a fast, high-precision service, which departed from Southampton each Thursday afternoon, for Capetown, Port Elizabeth, East London and Durban. With weekly sailings being run in each direction and throughout the year, no less than eight large liners, 'mailships' as they were called, were required. Mostly well over 20,000 tons, they carried comparatively few passengers, often as few as 700, but had considerable cargo space.*

In this scene, at Southampton in December 1958, Union-Castle's last twin-stacker, the 19,200-ton Arundel Castle *of 1921, is departing for a Far Eastern scrapyard. Finishing nearly four decades of service, this beloved old ship, a former four-stacker that had been modernized in the late thirties, was being replaced by a new generation of larger and faster 'mailships', the* Pendennis Castle *of 1958, then the* Windsor Castle *of 1960 and finally the* Transvaal Castle *of 1961. Beyond the* Arundel Castle *are two other Castle liners, the* Athlone Castle *and the aforementioned* Pendennis Castle. (Union Castle Line.)

Right *Unlike most large passenger liners, the Union-Castle ships relied heavily on cargo. Southbound, from either London on the round Africa route or from Southampton on the famed 'Cape Mail Express' to South Africa, the liners carried mostly manufactured goods— machinery, motor cars, appliances. Homeward, there would be gold, fruits and copper. Of course, the most important cargo of all was the swift, precision delivery of the mails in both directions. Large passenger ships such as the 28,629-ton* Pretoria Castle *had space for 154 first class passengers and 491 in tourist as well as over 8,000 tons of freight. In this scene, along the Southampton Docks, in June 1955, cargo is being loaded aboard the* Braemar Castle *in the foreground while beyond is the* Pretoria Castle, *in port between voyages to the South African Cape.* (Roger Sherlock.)

One of Britain's alternate passenger shippers to Africa was the British India Line. While most of their passenger fleet was, in fact, based at Indian ports and rarely visited home waters, the Company's largest liners, the sisters Kenya *(shown loading at Kilindini in Kenya) and* Uganda, *sailed to East Africa. Carrying two classes of passenger and considerable freight, they travelled from London to Gibraltar, Naples, Port Said, Aden, Mombasa, Tanga, Zanzibar, Dar-es-Salaam, Beira and then turned around at Durban. Following the decolonization of British East Africa in the late sixties, the very profitable social and economic ties that supported these ships diminished quite rapidly. The* Kenya *was scrapped subsequently while the* Uganda *was converted for a revived 'second career', as a schools cruiseship. (P&O Group.)*

In 1965 the traditional Thursday afternoon sailings of the big Union Castle liners from Southampton ceased. A new accelerated schedule was put into effect, in fact a gradual prelude to the demise of the entire passenger-mail service. Instead of the previous eight liners required, the sailing schedules were worked on an accelerated 11½-day run to Capetown (instead of the earlier thirteen days), using five passenger liners and two high-powered freighters. Right, on a summer's day along the Southampton Docks, in 1960, the brand new Union-Castle flagship Windsor Castle *(right) is preparing for her maiden sailing to South Africa. Just behind her is one of the older generation, the* Winchester Castle *of 1930, which is about to be retired and then scrapped. (Union-Castle Line.)*

Union-Castle's more extended passenger-cargo service were the round Africa voyages—the 'RA run' as it was called—which encircled continental Africa, either out by the West Coast or alternately from the East Coast. Ports of call 'out west' began at London, then Rotterdam and onwards to Las Palmas, Ascension, St Helena, Capetown, Port Elizabeth, East London, Durban, Lourenco Marques, Beira, Dar-es-Salaam, Zanzibar, Tanga, Mombasa, Aden, Port Sudan, Suez, Port Said, Genoa, Marseilles and Gibraltar, and then home to London. Occasional variations for special cargo or military reasons included Naples, Djibouti and ports in Portugese East Africa like Nacala. The entire round trip took about eight weeks. The last passenger ships especially built for this service were a 17,000-ton trio, the Rhodesia Castle *(shown right, arriving at Capetown for the first time in 1951),* Kenya Castle *and* Braemar Castle. *Each carried approximately 500 passengers, all of them in one-class accommodation. (John Havers Collection.)*

British India's base at Bombay was a very busy second homeport. There were passenger and cargo services out to East Africa and the Seychelles, as well as homeward to Britain. Another trade went to the Persian Gulf, using a 4,800-ton quartet of sisterships, the Dara, Daressa, Dumra *and* Dwarka. *After leaving Bombay they travelled to Karachi and then such Gulf ports as Gwadur, Muscat, Dubai, Umm Said, Bahrain, Bushire, Kuwait, Khorramshahr and Basrah. Their capacities reflected their unusual operation, with about sixty cabin passengers and the remainder, approximately 1,000, in unberthed, deck class. Consequently, aboard the same ship, on one of these steamy passages, their might be a Middle Eastern prince in cabin class and a migrant worker and his family in below-deck quarters. The* Dwarka, *shown right at Karachi, was the last of these ships and the last of British India's overseas passenger ships. She was retired and then scrapped in 1982. (P&O Group.)*

Above *On the Latin American route, long supported by southbound migrants, northbound meat cargoes and even a round trip 'cruise like' passenger clientele, one of the more unique services was Pacific Steam Navigation Company's run to the West Coast of South America. Their final passenger ship, the 21,500-ton* Reina del Mar, *shown departing on her maiden voyage from Liverpool, on 3 May 1956, plied a most extensive route. From Britain she then put into La Rochelle in France and then Santander and La Coruna in Spain before crossing to Bermuda, Nassau, Havana, Kingston, La Guaira, Curacao, Cartagena, Cristobal, La Libertad, Callao, Arica, Antofagasta and then a turnaround at Valparaiso. A three-class trade, with first class, cabin and tourist accommodation, it expired by 1963. The highly popular* Reina del Mar *found new life as a one-class cruiseship, sailing mostly for the Union-Castle Line. (Everett Viez Collection.)*

Left *After the Second World War, the transpacific passenger trades never quite regained their pre-war sparkle. Among others, the Japanese liners were all but missing, with only a single 11,000-tonner, the* Hikawa Maru, *still surviving. For some years, the largest and most important ships were the sisterships* President Cleveland *and* President Wilson *of the American President Lines. Laid down as post-war military transports, they were completed to a luxurious passenger standard, with accommodation in first and tourist class, ranging from superb de luxe suites in first to dormitories in tourist. Their sailings took them from San Francisco and Los Angeles to Honolulu and then to Yokohama, Kobe, Hong Kong and Manila. When finally withdrawn in early 1972, they ended the last regular liner service across the Pacific. Thereafter, there would be periodic sailings only, made mostly by cruiseships on 'positioning' voyages. (Everett Viez Collection.)*

Trooping by sea continued for some years after the Second World War, primarily with American and British ships. The Americans used mostly specially built transports, often with capacities as large as 4,000, that were built at the end of the war. Almost all were retired in the early seventies. The British fleet, usually older ships that carried as many as four classes, were often pre-war vessels. The Empire Fowey, *shown above as she departs from Southampton for the Far East, was the North German Lloyd's* Potsdam *of 1935. Built originally for the Hamburg-Suez-Orient run, she was seized during the Allied invasion of 1945 and then given a three-year conversion and rebuilding before entering British service, under the operational management of P&O. While Britain closed down their troopship services in 1964, the* Empire Fowey *was withdrawn several years earlier, in 1960, and sold off to Pakistani buyers for continued service as an Indian Ocean pilgrim ship. (P&O Group.)*

The Australian migrant trade was especially busy and profitable in the years following the Second World War. Among other reasons, Australia represented the opportunity for 'new life' with greater economic opportunity. The government itself sponsored a highly appealing fare-assisted programme, often for as little as £10, to Fremantle, Melbourne or Sydney. Along with such firms as P&O-Orient and Shaw Savill, others—particularly the Italians and Greeks—invested strongly as well. It was the ideal service for considerable profits; near-guaranteed outbound sailings that covered the costs of half-empty homeward runs. The Lauro Line, which began with two converted small aircraft carriers on the migrant trade, took a significant step in the mid sixties by purchasing two out-of-work Dutch liners, the* Oranje *of 1939 and the* Willem Ruys *from 1947, both formerly on the East Indies trade to Djakarta. Both were given very extensive conversions, major cosmetic surgery in fact, that resulted in almost unrecognizable 'new' ships. With new winged funnels, elaborate aft lido decks and swimming pools and redesigned, contemporary passenger quarters, the* Oranje *reappeared as the* Angelina Lauro *and the* Willem Ruys *as the* Achille Lauro (*shown here at Lisbon). With their capacities almost doubled, they had several profitable years ahead, before the Australian migrant contract went to an airline and both ships were transferred to full time cruising. It was in this role that the* Achille Lauro *achieved notoriety when she was hijacked by the Palestine Liberation Front in 1985. (Luis Miguel Correia.)*

Above *One of the most important and revolutionary ships of the pre-war era was Shaw Savill Line's* Southern Cross *of 1955, the first major liner to mount her engines and therefore her funnel far aft. This created not only free spaces in the midship passenger areas, but substantial open spaces along the top decks. A considerable success, the idea was soon copied by, among others, the Dutch for their new flagship* Rotterdam, *by P&O for their* Canberra *and by a Shaw Savill successor, the* Northern Star *of 1962. Furthermore, the* Southern Cross *was, at the time of her creation, the largest passenger liner to offer high standard all-tourist-class accommodation (for 1,100 passengers) and yet absolutely no provision for cargo. Routed on continuous 76-day around the world voyages, her customary itineraries departed from Southampton and then proceeded to Trinidad, Curacao, the Panama Canal, Fiji, Wellington, Sydney, Melbourne, Fremantle, Durban, Capetown and then to Las Palmas before returning home. She proved highly popular not only with Australian migrants and interport passengers, but developed a round trip following as well. (Everett Viez Collection.)*

Below left *The Greek-flag Chandris Lines also saw a very bright future in the post-war Australian migrant trade. In particular, they purchased a string of unprofitable American liners, such as Matson's* Lurline, *the United States Lines'* America *and later another* Lurline, *the former* Matsonia. *Taken in hand at the Company's private repair works near Piraeus, they were systematically and efficiently converted as all-tourist-class ships, again with capacities that were often more than doubled. Much like such companies as Italy's Lauro, Cogedar and Sitmar Lines, their ships were not routed purely through the Mediterranean, however. Their voyages often began at Bremerhaven, Rotterdam and Southampton, and then continued via Genoa, Naples and/or Piraeus, before continuing onward to Port Said, Aden, Colombo, Fremantle, Melbourne and Sydney (many sailings were extended to Auckland or Wellington, and then continued homeward to Europe via Fiji, the Panama Canal and Caribbean ports). Chandris ran the last schedule of low-fare migrant sailings, which were closed out at the end of 1977. Ships such as the* Britanis *sought new careers, returning to North American waters no less, as tropical cruiseships. (Luis Miguel Correia.)*

Above right *Among other smaller merchant fleets, the Argentines had several passenger ships built after the Second World War. A trio of high-standard combination passenger-cargo liners sailed to London, Le Havre and Hamburg, two migrant ships traded to Amsterdam and Hamburg, and two further migrant liners went into the Mediterranean, to Genoa, Naples and Barcelona. Three further ships, the sisterships* Rio de la Plata, Rio Jachal *(shown docking at New York) and* Rio Tunuyan, *had very fine all-first-class accommodation for 116 passengers as well as sizeable cargo capacities. They rotated their sailings, which were often sold as six-week full cruises, between New York, Trinidad, Rio de Janeiro, Santos, Montevideo and Buenos Aires. Like so many others by the early seventies, the full effects of aircraft competition sent these ships to the scrappers.* (Moran Towing & Transportation Company.)

Right *The Japanese seemed hardly interested in passenger shipping after the devastation of the Second World War. Without rebuilding their established link to the North American West Coast, they built two specially designed migrant passenger ships, the* Brazil Maru *of 1954 and the* Argentina Maru *of 1958 (shown sailing from Yokohama), for the Latin American route. Being basically of freighter design, there were twelve berths in first class, about sixty in a modified tourist class and then well over 900 in something akin to steerage. Carrying thousands of Japanese to 'new lives' in Brazil and Argentina especially, the ships plied a long-haul service between Kobe, Yokohama, Honolulu, Los Angeles, the Panama Canal, La Guaira, Rio de Janeiro, Santos, Montevideo and Buenos Aires. (Hisashi Noma Collection.)*

A sizeable number of older passenger ships and war-built vessels were used in post-war low-fare services. Some went out to Australia, Latin America, or South Africa with migrants, others carried refugees and dependents, and still others transported troops. A former freighter and then converted aircraft carrier, the West German Seven Seas, *a 12,500-tonner, was rebuilt to carry twenty passengers in a small, upper-deck first class and nearly 1,000 travellers in a rather spartan tourist class. She ran summer season transatlantic crossings, to either Montreal or New York from Rotterdam, Le Havre and Southampton, Australian voyages to Melbourne and Sydney, and—in later years—for two annual 'floating university' cruises with a complement of students and their instructors. (Europe-Canada Line.)*

While thought of mostly as a Caribbean cruiseship, the Grace Lines sisterships Santa Paula *and* Santa Rosa *were designed primarily for one-way passenger traffic between New York, the Caribbean and Venezuela, and for cargo service. Such combination ships derived their income (and profit) from several aspects of shipping service. In the scene below, the* Santa Rosa *is inbound to New York, on 26 March 1959, carrying a most unusual cargo; some decking and the funnel of the tanker* Valchem. *The two ships had collided in thick fog off the New Jersey coast. Such were the hazards of ship operations. After some prompt repairs at a Brooklyn shipyard, the* Santa Rosa—*barely missing a sailing—returned to her Caribbean schedule. (Moran Towing & Transportation Company.)*

Chapter 6

The great white cruiseships

Cruising, voyages of leisure rather than transport, have become the mainstay, the survival in fact, of ocean liners. While the first cruise-type voyage was offered in 1857, aboard P&O's *Ceylon*, it remained very much the domain of the very rich and the very adventurous. In the twenties, celebrated transatlantic liners such as the *Mauretania* and *France* went off on wintertime Mediterranean jaunts, carrying as few as 200 millionaires that were served by over 700 crew members. The thirties brought cruising to the general public, mostly because of the escapism such voyages provided in the face of the bleak Depression. In December 1936 the *Literary Digest* reported, 'Six years ago the "short" cruise was unknown'. Liners set off on overnight trips out to sea, 'cruises to nowhere', as well as long weekends to Bermuda and Nova Scotia, and on seven to fourteen-day runs to the Caribbean, the Canaries, Spain and Portugal and the Northern Cities.

After the Second World War, the Cunard Company built the first major liner purposely for cruising, the 34,000-ton *Caronia*. Painted in four shades of green and with private bathroom facilities throughout and a deckside pool, she was sent on long, luxurious trips throughout the year; around the world, around continental Africa, the Pacific and Far East, the Mediterranean and Black Seas, and the North Cape and Scandinavian cities. Rarely did the *Caronia* run short cruises. Her long cruise following was devoted, including many passengers who booked voyage after voyage and others who 'lived' aboard for several years. One passenger, Clara McBeth of New York, remained on the ship for some fifteen years (except during dry-dock periods, of course) and is reputed to have

paid Cunard some $20 million in fares. Some years later, during the 1960s, another British liner, Royal Mail's *Andes*, developed a very similar loyal following. The ship, with only 480 berths that were looked after by 500 hand-picked staff members, became akin to a floating country club, the 'Club *Andes*' in fact. Many passengers, who came year after year, requested not only the same stateroom (or suite) with the same attending steward and stewardess, but the same restaurant table with the same waiter. A strong sense of regularity was a highpoint to travelling in the *Andes*. One staff member recalled later, that to almost all passenger requests, the response had to be 'Yes, madam' or 'Yes, sir'.

Because of the post-war boom period of regular liner services, be it on the North Atlantic or to South America or Australia, few ships went cruising. At New York, only in the deep winter months did such ships as the *Mauretania, Nieuw Amsterdam* and *Kungsholm* set off on West Indian trips. By early spring, they would return to the more demanding, more profitable 'line voyages' across the Atlantic. Among the regular cruise-like voyages being offered from New York on a full time basis were the ships of the Grace, Moore McCormack and Panama lines. While actually combination passenger-cargo liners that relied heavily on one-way, inter-port passenger traffic as well as substantial amounts of cargo, the companies offered the round trip sailings, from two to six weeks, as cruise voyages. The Grace liners offered two-week trips on their 300-passenger *Santa Rosa* and *Santa Paula*, eighteen- to nineteen-day 'freighter style' cruises on their 52-passenger *Santa Clara, Santa Monica* and *Santa Sofia* and 40- to 42-day runs to the West Coast of South America as far as Chile on additional 52-passenger combo ships, the *Santas Barbara, Cecilia, Isabel, Luisa, Margarita* and *Maria*. Moore-McCormack ran monthly round-trips to the South American Atlantic coast, to Trinidad, Rio de Janeiro, Santos, Montevideo and turnaround at Buenos Aires. The Panama Line, while created as a supply link to the Canal Zone, sensibly offered 14-day cruise voyages as well in their three all first class vessels *Ancon, Cristobal* and *Panama*. Passengers enjoyed extended stays in port, a result of the considerable cargo handling, at Cristobal and at Port-au-Prince in each direction.

During the fifties a number of unknown companies attempted to enter the short cruise trades. Unfortunately many of them used very old, ill-suited tonnage that failed rather quickly. Others were more successful, such as the Eastern Steamship Lines of Miami which employed the 5,000-ton former coastal liners *Evangeline* and *Yarmouth* on Bahamas and Caribbean voyages. With limited competition it didn't quite matter that the public rooms were dated, the staterooms small, the deck spaces cramped and the swimming pool perched just over the stern. On the New York run the newly formed Incres Line transformed the ageing P&O liner *Mongolia*, built in 1923 and which later sailed as the *Rimutaka* for the New Zealand Shipping Company, as the cruiseship *Nassau*. Modernized, painted overall in tropic whites and blues and rebuilt in the stern section with a vast lido deck and twin pools, she was sent on weekly cruises to Nassau, seven days for £61 ($170). Her success

was considerable and was the beginning of continuous, year-round cruise voyages that would become the main staple of the ocean liner industry by the sixties and seventies. The *Nassau* was soon followed by another remodelled liner, Home Lines' *Italia*, built originally in 1928 as the Swedish *Kungsholm*, but refaced with pools, lido decks, air conditioning and a generally festive atmosphere. She too plied the weekly Nassau trade.

The Furness-Bermuda Lines, a division of Britain's Furness Withy Group, was also an important pioneer in the year-round cruise trades. Their ships, the pre-war *Queen of Bermuda* and her post-war running-mate, the smaller *Ocean Monarch*, sailed from New York each Saturday on the forty-hour runs to Bermuda. They remained in port for nearly three days and then returned to the United States. While some passengers made the round trip (six days for £50 ($140), in the late fifties), others elected to stay ashore for a time and then return on a subsequent sailing. Still others sailed southbound on the *Queen of Bermuda* and then transferred to the *Ocean Monarch* for the homeward voyage. Sailing from New York with precision regularity on most Saturdays, at three in the afternoon, they became especially popular with the 'just married' set and became known as the 'honeymoon ships'.

By the early sixties, the wintertime cruise offerings from New York were quite abundant and diverse, as shown in this schedule from 1960:

Ship	Date	Rates	Itinerary
Empress of Britain	13 February	$350	14-day Caribbean, 5 ports
Bianca C	16 February	$435	16-day Caribbean, 8 ports
Independence	16 February	$815	23-day Mediterranean, 10 ports
Empress of England	19 February	$475	19-day Caribbean, 9 ports
Nassau	19 February	$250	10-day Nassau & Port-au-Prince
Santa Paula	19 February	$595	13-day Caribbean, 6 ports
Nieuw Amsterdam	19 February	$515	17-day Caribbean, 8 ports
Santa Clara	19 February	$595	18-day Caribbean, 6 ports
Brasil	19 February	$1,350	31-day South American, 9 ports
Rio Jachal	19 February	$1,080	43-day South American, 8 ports
Queen of Bermuda	20 February	$225	9-day Bermuda & Nassau
Cristobal	24 February	$360	14-day Caribbean, 3 ports
Hanseatic	25 February	$420	15-day Caribbean, 6 ports
Mauretania	25 February	$525	18-day Caribbean, 7 ports
Santa Rosa	26 February	$595	13-day Caribbean, 6 ports
Victoria	26 February	$555	17-day Caribbean, 8 ports
Santa Monica	26 February	$595	18-day Caribbean, 6 ports
Jerusalem	27 February	$315	13-day Caribbean, 6 ports
Statendam	27 February	$375	13-day Caribbean, 5 ports
Bremen	27 February	$395	14-day Caribbean, 7 ports
Constitution	27 February	$815	23-day Mediterranean, 9 ports

Ship	Date	Rates	Itinerary
Empress of Britain	29 February	$350	14-day Caribbean, 6 ports
Homeric	29 February	$485	16-day Caribbean, 7 ports
Queen of Bermuda	1 March	$225	9-day Bermuda & Nassau
Ancon	1 March	$360	14-day Caribbean, 3 ports
Nassau	4 March	$170	7-day Nassau
Bianca C	4 March	$310	12-day Caribbean, 4 ports
Santa Paula	4 March	$595	13-day Caribbean, 6 ports
Santa Sofia	4 March	$595	18-day Caribbean, 6 ports
Gripsholm	8 March	$1,565	50-day Mediterranean, 26 ports
Nieuw Amsterdam	9 March	$435	14-day Caribbean, 7 ports
Empress of England	9 March	$475	19-day Caribbean, 9 ports
Queen of Bermuda	11 March	$167	7-day Bermuda
Nassau	11 March	$170	7-day Nassau
Santa Rosa	11 March	$595	13-day Caribbean, 6 ports
Santa Clara	11 March	$595	18-day Caribbean, 6 ports
Argentina	11 March	$1,110	31-day South American, 9 ports
Cristobal	11 March	$360	14-day Caribbean, 3 ports
Rio Tunuyan	11 March	$1,080	43-day South American, 8 ports
Jerusalem	12 March	$285	12-day Caribbean, 5 ports
Independence	12 March	$1,395	40-day Mediterranean, 13 ports
Hanseatic	14 March	$345	13-day Caribbean, 4 ports
Statendam	14 March	$390	14-day Caribbean, 8 ports
Victoria	15 March	$460	14-day Caribbean, 6 ports
Bianca C	17 March	$310	12-day Caribbean, 4 ports
Ancon	17 March	$360	14-day Caribbean, 3 ports
Mauretania	18 March	$415	14-day Caribbean, 8 ports
Exeter	18 March	$1,070	41-day Mediterranean, 13 ports
Nassau	18 March	$170	7-day Nassau
Santa Paula	18 March	$595	13-day Caribbean, 6 ports
Santa Monica	18 March	$595	18-day Caribbean, 6 ports
Homeric	18 March	$425	15-day Caribbean, 6 ports
Queen of Bermuda	19 March	$153	6-day Bermuda

The average exchange rate for 1960 was $2.81 to £1.

Cruising from British ports began to expand by the mid sixties, especially as many of the older liners were being replaced by new tonnage and as the very first signs of aircraft competition began to appear. The British cruise industry also faced intense rivalry from 'sun flights', inexpensive air junkets to holiday spots in Spain, Majorca, Malta, North Africa and even in Yugoslavia and Greece. A week's tour might cost as little as £50 ($140). A sample listing of British-based cruises during the winter of 1965–66 included:

Ship	Date	Rates	Itinerary
Chitral	9 November	£478	74-day Far Eastern, 18 ports
Transvaal Castle	12 November	£273	38-day South African, 10 ports
Arkadia	12 November	£91	14-day Canary Islands, 7 ports
Prins der Nederlanden	13 November	£206	34-day Caribbean, 8 ports
Uruguay Star	*13 November	£356	47-day South American, 11 ports
Orsova	*14 November	£310	68-day Australian, 21 ports
Andes	15 November	£213	23-day Caribbean, 4 ports
Flandre	16 November	£245	21-day Caribbean, 9 ports
Golfito	17 November	£228	25-day Caribbean, 2 ports
Pendennis Castle	19 November	£215	38-day South African, 10 ports
Arlanza	*19 November	£259	46-day South American, 14 ports
Aureol	**19 November	£245	30-day West African, 10 ports
Oranjestad	19 November	£171	38-day South American, 6 ports
Oranjefontein	20 November	£180	57-day South African, 11 ports

Ship	Date	Rates	Itinerary
Hannover	21 November	£608	98-day Far Eastern, 21 ports
City of Port Elizabeth	*23 November	£351	65-day South African, 13 ports
Irpinia	25 November	£241	28-day Caribbean, 16 ports
Antilles	25 November	£245	21-day Caribbean, 9 ports
Paraguay Star	*27 November	£356	47-day South American, 11 ports
Camito	1 December	£228	25-day Caribbean, 2 ports
Pretoria Castle	3 December	£200	38-day South African, 10 ports
Denbighshire	*3 December	£478	88-day Far Eastern, 13 ports
Apapa	**3 December	£245	31-day West African, 10 ports
Iberia Star	*4 December	£372	47-day South American, 11 ports
Oranje Nassau	4 December	£206	34-day Caribbean, 8 ports
Oriana	5 December	£310	50-day Australian, 15 ports
Chusan	5 December	£658	110-day around the world, 29 ports
Angelina Lauro	6 December	£329	65-day Australian, 24 ports
Southern Cross	9 December	£386	76-day around the world, 12 ports
Windsor Castle	10 December	£231	38-day South African, 10 ports
Amazon	*10 December	£259	46-day South American, 14 ports
Willemstad	10 December	£171	38-day South American, 6 ports
City of Exeter	*14 December	£369	65-day South African, 13 ports
Golfito	15 December	£228	25-day Caribbean, 2 ports
Accra	**17 December	£245	30-day West African, 10 ports
Arkadia	17 December	£72	11-day Canary Islands, 4 ports
Capetown Castle	17 December	£68	11-day Canary Islands, 3 ports
Jagersfontein	18 December	£180	57-day South African, 11 ports
Brasil Star	*18 December	£356	47-day South American, 11 ports
Schwabenstein	19 December	£608	99-day Far Eastern, 21 ports
Andes	19 December	£157	17-day West African, 3 ports
Empress of England	**20 December	£130	17-day Atlantic Isles, 5 ports
Venus	21 December	£107	14-day Atlantic Isles, 6 ports
France	21 December	£148	13-day West Africa, 4 ports
Sylvania	**22 December	£85	12-day Atlantic Isles, 5 ports
Antilles	22 December	£305	28-day Caribbean, 12 ports
Arcadia	22 December	£79	11-day Atlantic Isles, 3 ports
Kenya Castle	*23 December	£291	62-day East Africa, 15 ports
Irpinia	24 December	£70	12-day Atlantic Isles, 6 ports
Edinburgh Castle	24 December	£219	38-day South African, 10 ports
Capetown Castle	28 December	£86	14-day Atlantic Isles, 5 ports
Arkadia	28 December	£85	13-day Atlantic Isles, 7 ports
Camito	29 December	£228	25-day Caribbean, 2 ports
Aureol	**31 December	£245	30-day West African, 10 ports
Aragon	*31 December	£259	47-day South American, 14 ports
Transvaal Castle	31 December	£296	38-day South African, 10 ports
Statendam	31 December	£99	14-day Atlantic Isles, 5 ports
Dinteldyk	**1 January	£390	85-day North American West Coast, 20 ports
Argentina Star	**1 January	£387	47-day South American, 11 ports
Orcades	**1 January	£364	75-day Australian, 17 ports

Cruises marked * sailed from London and those marked ** sailed from Liverpool. All other cruises departed from Southampton.

The average exchange rate for 1965 was $2.80 to £1.

One of the more novel—and successful—of the British based cruise operations was British India Line's 'educational cruise' programme. Early ships, such as the converted troopers *Dunera*, *Devonia* and *Nevasa*, and then later the highly popular *Uganda*, were refitted to carry 200–300 adult passengers, usually in the former first class quarters, and then as many as 900 youngsters, mostly in specially fitted dormitory accommodation. While the ships travelled to more unique ports, often linked to a specific educational theme, a group of lecturers would travel aboard and offer some exceptional talks and presentations. Revived in the mid sixties (educational cruises had been offered in the thirties, during the slack season for British troopships) it endured for nearly two decades. When the last of these specialized ships, the 17,000-ton *Uganda*, was called to duty by the British Government for the Falklands War, it became the ideal opportunity to suspend operations. The student following had declined considerably by then, a consequence of ever-increasing inflation, while the loyal adult passengers were unable to singly support the ship's operational expenses.

By the mid sixties, as the North Atlantic trade slipped into its final phase, elderly ships— including the Cunard Queens—were detoured to cruising. At best, they were brief, ill thought-out attempts to keep such liners in service. Far too large and requiring deep drafts, they were unable to enter some of the smaller sunshine ports and therefore passengers had to endure long, uncomfortable tender rides ashore. Furthermore, the ships themselves lacked the essential provisions for the cruise trade, especially in American waters. The *Queen Mary*, for example, was only partially air-conditioned, without top deck pools, and had limited deck chair space. Her interior was wood-panelled and dark, not in keeping with a 'fun in the sun' image.

Cunard spent a million pounds on the *Queen Elizabeth* during her winter overhaul of 1965–66. A large lido with pool was fitted in the stern, private plumbing was extended to most of her cabins, full air-conditioning added and some of the lounges redone in more festive stylings with coloured lights, plastic flowers and potted ferns. In all it did little to improve the financially-ailing state of the aged liner. Most passengers remembered her as a prestige transatlantic ship, not as a sleek tropical cruise liner. For the few cruises that followed, most of her passengers were the curious and the nostalgic, many of them wanting a trip in a 'legendary dinosaur'. The newer *United States*, still the Blue Riband champion, faced similar problems when her owners sent her on one- and two-week Caribbean junkets. She was never intended to go into warm weather areas and lacked the suitable amenities. It should be made clear, however, that many former transatlantic liners made quite successful transitions into the cruise trades; the *Homeric, Nieuw Amsterdam, Gripsholm* and *Bergensfjord*, to name but a few.

Home Lines' *Oceanic*, a 39,200-tonner designed originally for the North Atlantic trade between Northern Europe and the St Lawrence, was commissioned in April 1965 as the first brand new large liner especially for the short cruise trades. To some shippers, running a 1,200-passenger ship on year-round trips between New York and Nassau could not be profitable. In fact it was a tremendous success and soon prompted other firms not only to close examine the superbly designed and decorated *Oceanic*, but consider short cruising as their future employment. The Norwegians were more than impressed. Beginning in the late sixties they commissioned one white cruise liner after another, larger, with more berths and better fitted, for what they saw as the biggest and busiest cruise area in the world, the Caribbean. The Norwegian Caribbean Lines, advertised as the first fleet of the Caribbean, added the *Sunward* in 1966, the *Starward* in 1968, the *Skyward* in 1969 and then the *Southward* in 1971. They had not been in the passenger ship trade previously. A Norwegian rival soon appeared, the Royal Caribbean Cruise Lines, which produced three sisters, the *Song of Norway, Nordic Prince* and *Sun Viking*, between 1970 and 1972. All of these ships were created for the one-week trade to such ports as Nassau, San Juan and St Thomas, or to the western Caribbean, to Montego Bay, Grand Cayman and Cozumel. As a strong 'repeat' clientele developed, extended cruises of ten to fourteen days were added as well, most of which reached deeper into the Caribbean and to Venezuela and Colombia.

The Norwegians presently own the most important cruise fleet in the world. Another firm, the Royal Viking Line, saw healthy days ahead for long-distance, luxury trips and built a trio of 550-passenger sisterships, the *Royal Viking Star, Royal Viking Sky* and *Royal Viking Sea*. Published in a thick booklet known as an 'atlas', the Royal Viking schedules are the most diverse in the cruise industry: ranging from two weeks to the Mexican Riviera, the St Lawrence and Alaska; six weeks in the Mediterranean or around South America; and a hundred days around the world. Like the earlier *Caronia* and *Andes*, they have developed a very loyal following, including some passengers who have booked voyage after voyage and one who has even moved some of her personal furnishings into a suite.

While this new generation of cruiseships entered service, some of the older ships managed to survive, often well beyond their expected lifetimes. The Costa Line's *Franca C*, the first cruiseship to be linked with an air-sea travel plan, in the Caribbean in 1968, remained in cruising until 1977, then aged 63! Another Italian, Grimaldi-Siosa Lines' *Irpinia*, was still cruising in the Mediterranean at the time of her fiftieth birthday in 1979. The Chandris liner *Britanis*, the former Matson liner *Monterey* of 1931, remains in service at the time of writing, running a variety of cruises ranging from £22.50 ($29) 'luncheon' cruises that sail just after breakfast and return just before dinner to five-day hops around the Caribbean. Others include another Chandris liner *The Victoria*, which is the vastly altered *Dunnottar Castle* from 1936, and the Eastern Steamship Lines' *Emerald Seas*, built in 1944 and now in her sixth life.

By the mid seventies, as the cruise industry intensified, became more and more profitable and therefore more competitive, the ocean liner industry of the past began to disappear rapidly. Those liner berths at New York were mostly empty, filled only on weekends with seven-day cruiseships bound for Bermuda or Nassau. The sixty liner berths of the transatlantic era in the fifties had become six berths for the remaining cruiseships. By 1984 the New York passenger piers were closed completely for the first time during the winter months. The biggest concentration of cruiseships in North America has moved to Miami, which is geographically well suited to overnight runs to the Bahamas and then quite near the sought-after Caribbean islands. Well over ninety per cent of the cruise traffic on American-based ships are flown into embarkation ports. Other busy cruise ports include Port Everglades, Tampa, New Orleans, Los Angeles, San Francisco and Vancouver (the latter for summertime Alaska cruises).

The directors of the Holland-America Line, for example, could not have imagined that soon after their last liner visit to Rotterdam in 1971 the company ships would be based in the United States and even using a Connecticut headquarters. In 1983 they relocated to Seattle to intensify their prime tourist business, the summer trade to Alaska. While the *Rotterdam* was one of the last 'ships of state' designed for the North Atlantic with only wintertime cruising, she has been cruising full time since the late sixties. After her wintertime ninety-day world cruise she spends the spring in the Caribbean, sailing from Florida. Passing through the Panama Canal, she then relocates to Vancouver for weekly passages through Alaska's Inside Passage and to such ports as Ketchikan, Juneau and Sitka. In the autumn she returns to the Caribbean. The company's newest liners, the 33,800-ton sistership *Nieuw Amsterdam* and

Noordam of 1983–84, have never even visited Holland and spend the entire year in American cruising.

In March 1977, at her New York pierside naming ceremony, Cunard confidently predicted that their 17,000-ton *Cunard Princess* would be the last brand new cruiseship. Others had similar thoughts and felt that the American cruise industry had reached its peak. This was not so, however, and within a short time it began to show further growth. However, the increase was not quite enough to warrant building brand new liners, which were then costing upwards of £57 million ($100 million) each. Some resourceful companies, namely the Royal Caribbean Cruise Line and Royal Viking Line, sent their ships to drydock for extensive overhauls that included the insertion of 90 ft 'midbodies' that increased their capacities (and therefore met the increasing demands for cruise space) by as much as 400 berths each. Three ships could be 'stretched' for £57 million ($100 million). The Norwegian Caribbean Lines reached in a different (and very bold) direction, however. They bought the idle 66,000-ton *France*, laid up for five years at Le Havre as a 'white elephant'. While most superliners, including the *United States*, *Michelangelo* and *Raffaello* which were also laid up, were thought to be destined only for the scrapyards, the Norwegians saw better days ahead for the biggest of them all. Spending a total of £56 million ($130 million) in the entire transformation, the *France* reappeared as the *Norway*, the complete Caribbean cruiseship. The enclosed spaces of the transatlantic era were replaced with broad sun decks, two pools, open-air bars, television in every stateroom, two decks of shops, a large disco, Las Vegas-style entertainment and Broadway theatre, and even an ice cream shop. By 1984, four years after her reintroduction, the *Norway* is earning a profit.

By the early eighties the cruise industry, again mostly in the United States, reached a staggering £2 billion ($4 billion) level. Several companies rushed to build bigger, better and more expensive ships. Between July 1983 and November 1984, the Holland America Line commissioned the *Nieuw Amsterdam* and *Noordam*, costing £243 million ($160 million) each; Sitmar added the 46,200-ton *Fairsky*; and P&O-Princess Cruises added the most expensive British liner ever, the 44,200-ton, £250 million ($165 million) *Royal Princess*. At the time of writing one shipping magazine has reported that there might be as many as two dozen cruise liners on the drawing boards, several of which are in the

50,000-ton range. Most importantly, however, is the Norwegian Caribbean Lines projected *Phoenix* scheme, a 200,000-ton cruiseship with 4–5,000 berths that would cost £390 million ($500 million). Rarely, if ever, visiting ports, she would be a self-contained 'floating resort' with pools, 'underwater bars' (bars below the water-line with viewing windows), extensive sporting facilities and even a skating rink. Passengers would reach the ship by large tenders and possibly even helicopters. While financing for the biggest, most expensive passenger ship ever is being organized, a German shipyard at Kiel is already seriously bidding for the construction, with delivery by the late eighties.

While the days of the *Normandie*, the *Rex* and the *Queen Mary*, those class-divided 'ships of state' that provided luxurious transport between continents, are long gone, the age and style of the ocean liner lives on. The new cruiseships, while not quite as charismatic or historic, continue the process of providing the most matchless vacation of all; a sea voyage. The sound of a deep whistle, those cheering moments between passengers and well-wishers on the dockside and that special thrill as the ship is released from shore and begins her voyage is still much the same as it was when the *Normandie* cast off from Le Havre or New York, the *Stratheden* from London or Sydney or the *Windsor Castle* from Capetown. Liners have indeed been the most marvellous moving objects made by man.

One of the pioneer ships of luxury cruising was Furness-Bermuda Line's Queen of Bermuda, *commissioned in 1933, used as troopship during the war and then restored by 1949. In the fifties, carrying 731 all-first-class passengers, she ran continuous six-day cruises from New York to Bermuda. She would depart, with the regularity of stop-watch accuracy, on Saturday afternoons at 15:00, reach her berth at Hamilton by Monday morning and then sail on Wednesday afternoon for the return passage to New York. The round trip voyage would conclude on Friday mornings. Fares began at £54 ($150) by the late fifties. (Todd Shipyards.)*

Below *Occasionally, the* Queen of Bermuda *would detour for an extended cruise, eight-days to both Bermuda and Nassau. Unlike subsequent cruiseships, she did have a cargo role as well. Among other goods, she delivered large quantities of fresh water to Bermuda. Her running-mate, the smaller 13,500-ton* Ocean Monarch, *built in 1951, ran Bermuda sailings as well, but was often used on more extensive trips such as two-week summer voyages to the St Lawrence and Canadian Maritimes, and special runs to the Caribbean islands. When cruising from American ports began to develop strongly, in the early sixties, veteran companies such as Furness-Bermuda with their older ships quickly fell out of step. In 1966, both the* Queen of Bermuda *and* Ocean Monarch *were retired and replaced by a brand new, sleek generation of cruiseships. (Everett Viez Collection.)*

Bottom *In the fifties, with the cruise trades in their infancy, many smaller, short-lived operations attempted to create tropical services. Unfortunately, many of these were with very old, ill-equipped ships. The Caribbean Cruise Lines of Miami took the* Tradewind, *a veteran from 1906 that had been the Ward Line's* Mexico *and then the Alaskan steamer* Aleutian, *for sailings to the Bahamas in the early fifties. Far from successful, the 6,200-ton liner was soon withdrawn and later finished her days in a Belgian scrapyard. (Everett Viez Collection.)*

Above left *One of the most successful older passenger ships transformed for cruising was P&O's* Mongolia, *dating from 1923. Bought by the Incres Line, a new entry in passenger shipping in the early fifties, she was totally refitted as the* Nassau. *There were lido decks, twin swimming pools and air-conditioned passenger quarters. For a decade she ran weekly cruises between New York and Nassau, with sailings usually on Friday evenings, just after business hours. Occasional holiday cruises were extended to Havana or Port-au-Prince. In her last cruise, which began in 1962, the* Nassau *reappeared as Mexico's first cruiseship, the* Acapulco, *the first liner to attempt regular cruises from Los Angeles to the Mexican Riviera. (Everett Viez Collection.)*

Above right *The New York based Grace Line was among the earlier and best known cruiseship firms. With interests centring around Latin America, their original* Santa Paula *and* Santa Rosa, *built in 1932, were retired and replaced in 1958 by a brand new pair with the same, highly popular names. Technically classified as combination passenger-cargo ships, with four large cargo holds each, these ships had luxurious provision for 300 first class passengers as well. They ran an exact service; departing from New York each Friday afternoon for a thirteen-day round trip to Curacao, La Guaira, Aruba, Kingston, Nassau and Port Everglades. In addition, Grace also ran nine 52-passenger combination ships on eighteen-day extended Caribbean cruises as well as longer voyages, of as much as six weeks, to the West Coast of South America as far as Valparaiso. (Everett Viez Collection.)*

Left *One of the best known companies serving the East Coast of South America was another American, the Moore McCormack Lines, also based at New York. In 1958, they replaced their pre-war liners with two very fine, all-first class cruiseships, the* Argentina *and* Brasil. *Boasting some of the largest staterooms ever to go to sea as well as twin pools, a solarium in the dummy smoke-stack and 'round-the-clock full cabin service, they ran mostly on the long-haul route of about thirty days, to Trinidad, Rio de Janeiro, Santos, Montevideo and Buenos Aires. In later years they travelled also to Africa, the Mediterranean and Scandinavia.* (Everett Viez Collection.)

Above right *As the transatlantic liner trades began to decline steadily by the early sixties, more and more ships were detoured to cruising, often making fewer transocean passages and given extended schedules to the tropics. During those years, especially in the week or so prior to the Christmas holidays, there would be impressive gatherings of Caribben-bound cruiseships along 'Luxury Liner Row', in a manner similar to those earlier scenes of the transatlantic ships in formation. In this view, from the late sixties, there are seven liners at berth: the Greek Line's* Queen Anna Maria *at top; then Cunard's* Franconia, *North German Lloyd's* Bremen, *the Incres Line's* Victoria, *the Italian Line's* Michelangelo *and Canadian Pacific's* Empress of Canada. *At the slip closest in view is the most popular cruiseship of the time, the Home Lines'* Oceanic. (Port Authority of New York & New Jersey.)

Right *As the old North Atlantic trade was finally reduced to a single liner, Cunard's* Queen Elizabeth 2, *which sailed for about half the year to Cherbourg and Southampton, New York City's well-known passenger liner docks were restricted to a mere six berths. They were occupied mostly by Bermuda- and Nassau-bound cruiseships and then all but deserted in the bleak winter months, especially as most liners departed for the warm-weather water homeports such as Miami, Port Ever-glades and San Juan. Three of the original transatlantic terminals were rebuilt, at a cost of some £14 million ($35 million), and then reopened in the autumn of 1974. In this scene, from a Saturday morning in the following June, a time which would have witnessed considerable Atlantic departures in previous decades, there were six liners at berth. Only one, Italy's* Michelangelo, *that was bound for Europe. Even she was to be retired shortly thereafter. From left to right, there is Norwegian America Line's* Sagafjord; *Home Lines'* Doric; *the* Michelangelo; *Home Lines'* Oceanic; *and two Holland-America liners, the* Rotterdam *and* Staten-dam. (Port Authority of New York & New Jersey.)

Nassau had long been one of the most popular cruiseship ports of call. In this dramatic aerial scene, from February 1975, there are six liners at dock. The Soviet Union's Maksim Gorky *is about to dock, adjacent to P&O's* Oronsay *and Home Lines'* Oceanic. *In the background, at the slightly smaller berths, is the Costa Line's* Flavia *on the left, and the running-mates* Emerald Seas *and* Bahama Star *of the Eastern Steamship Lines. Over 4,300 passengers went ashore that day—for shopping, island tours and long afternoons at the beach. (Everett Viez Collection.)*

The most important cruiseship of the sixties was Home Lines' 39,200-ton Oceanic, *commissioned in the spring of 1965. While originally intended for a transatlantic run between Hamburg, the Channel ports and Montreal, she was promptly rerouted and modified, in view of pressing competition from jet aircraft at the time, for year-round weekly cruises between New York and Nassau. It was a bold venture at the time, especially considering the clientele needed to support a 1,200-passenger vessel on a weekly basis. It was, in fact, a huge success, and soon spurned a new generation of other large cruiseships. Among other features, the* Oceanic—*with her twin upper-deck pools placed amidships—used a Magrodome, a sliding glass dome that cover the entire lido deck and pool area in as little as two minutes. Coupled with superb decor and highly reputed Italian service and cuisine, the* Oceanic *was for well over a decade the most popular and successful cruise liner afloat. (Everett Viez Collection.)*

While the Caribbean has been the busiest and most profitable cruising area in the world, the Mediterranean has also proved to be particularly popular. Especially popular are fly'n'sail package cruises, where travellers are delivered by aircraft to such ports of embarkation as Genoa, Villefranche, Barcelona, Palma, Venice and Athens for one- and two-week voyages. Older ships have found 'new lives' in these trades along with a brand new, specially built generation. In this scene at Malta's Valetta Harbour, on 5 October 1970, four major cruiseships are in port together. The Mermoz of France's Paquet Cruises is at anchor in the foreground. Just arriving, in the centre position, is British India's Uganda, an educational cruiseship with accommodation for 300 adults and 900 youngsters. In the background, both at anchorage, the Chandris Queen Frederica (although wearing Sovereign Cruises' logos, the ship's charterers) is on the left; the Soviet Taras Schevchenko, chartered to the West Germans, is to the right. (P&O Group.)

Even the remote Far East included some cruise voyages, departing from the likes of Yokohama, Hong Kong, Singapore, Sydney and Auckland. In this view, taken at Yokohama on 22 March 1973, the Swedish American Line's Kungsholm is at dock as part of her 90-day around the world cruise. Just before her is the Hong Kong based Coral Princess, operated by the China Navigation Company. A Soviet passenger ship, the Baikal, is berthed just to the left of the Kungsholm's forward funnel. (R. Izawa.)

Above *Some of the most celebrated cruiseships belonged to the Swedish American Line. With their normal capacities halved to about 400 passengers, who were served by an equal number of hand-picked staff members, beautifully decorated and exquisitely maintained ships such as the 27,000-ton* Kungsholm *of 1966 followed much of an established pattern: around the world or throughout the Far East in January; springtime in Europe and the British Isles; summers in Scandinavia; and then autumn to the Mediterranean, around Africa or around South America. Loyal passengers came year after year, often on the same cruise, and at least one millionairess enjoyed reserving an entire deck for her family, friends and staff. Shown during one of her shorter cruises, a six-day run to Bermuda, the* Kungsholm *ran in latter years for Norwegian owners, Flagship Cruises of Oslo, but with Liberian registry. Presently, she sails as P&O's* Sea Princess. *(Everett Viez Collection.)*

Left *Another celebrated and highly prestigious Scandinavian cruiseship Norwegian America Line's* Sagafjord, *commissioned in 1965, was intended originally to spend part of her year on summer time transatlantic crossings. She rarely ever made such trips. Instead, she went almost directly into year-round cruise sailings; the Caribbean, Scandinavia, the Mediterranean and even three-month trips around the world or throughout the Pacific. In the latter seventies, as the North American cruise industry fell into a temporary slump, the* Sagafjord *was briefly sent into lay-up. However, she later resumed sailing—and with her impeccable image intact. By the early eighties she was judged by at least one important travel guide to be finest cruise liner afloat. (J. F. Rodriguez.)*

Of course, not all cruiseliners enjoyed unlimited success and popularity. In the early seventies, as fuel oil costs suddenly rocketed and then prompted dramatic increases in passage fares, many ships fell on hard times. In this rather poetic scene at Southampton in 1972, three out-of-work liners are nested together, awaiting new owners and future service. The Southern Cross (far left), owned by Shaw Savill, later found life with the Greeks, becoming the Calypso for the Ulysses Lines. Cunard's Carmania and Franconia went to the Soviets, who had them refitted for charter cruising as the Leonid Sobinov and Feodor Shalypain. (Solent News Agency.)

American cruiseships began to disappear rapidly by the early seventies. Victims of staggering operational costs, many were laid up at first and then, with the proper Government clearances in hand, were sold off to foreign owners. Moore McCormack's Argentina and Brasil had barely a decade of service under Yankee colours before being sent to the backwaters of Baltimore in the autumn of 1969. Four years later, they were sold to the Holland-America Line and taken to Bremerhaven for thorough refitting as the Caribbean cruiseships Veendam and Volendam. (Moore McCormack Lines.)

Above left *It would seem that the most newsworthy liner of recent years has been, in fact, the supposed 'last of the superliners', Cunard's 67,000-ton* Queen Elizabeth 2. *Completed in the spring of 1969, she has suffered a string of misfortunes; breakdowns at sea, small fires, groundings, bomb hoaxes and even a mid-ocean transfer of her passengers and crew to another liner. For about six months of each year, she sails the traditional routeing, on the North Atlantic between New York, Cherbourg and Southampton, but with about 1,700 single-class passengers that enjoy mostly cruiseship-like comforts and amenities. For the remainder of the year, she cruises 'to the sun'—from overnight jaunts out to sea, to one-week runs to the Caribbean, to three months around the world starting each January.* (Cunard Line.)

Above right *In late 1978, during a refit at a New York Harbor shipyard, two duplex penthouse suites were added to the QE2. They have since rated as the most expensive accommodation ever to go to sea. For the 1985 winter world cruise, this accommodation was priced at over £266,000 ($300,000).* (Cunard Line.)

Above far right *One of the most popular forms of ocean cruising, particularly from British ports, was the British India Line's educational cruising programme. Ships such as the converted troopship* Nevasa *were divided between approximately 300 adult passengers, housed in the former first class quarters, and then some 900 youngsters, travelling mostly in large dormitories. Some of the best lecturers were brought aboard to enhance these sailings. Excursions followed suit—from archeological digs in Greece to mountain walks in Scotland to tours around deserted monasteries in Spain. Unfortunately, the concept became a victim of increasing inflation, especially as youngsters and their families could no longer afford these voyages. The last trips were run in 1983.* (P&O Group.)

Right *One out-of-work transatlantic liner, Canadian Pacific's* Empress of Canada *of 1961, was renamed* Mardi Gras *and took up a new career with a newly-formed, unknown firm, the Carnival Cruise Lines of Miami, in 1972. It was the beginning of one of the most successful firms in the North American industry, sailing first to the Caribbean and then extended services to the West Coast. Using Panamanian registry, their profits soon led to the acquisition of two other former British liners, the* Empress of Britain, *which sailed for a time as the Greek* Queen Anna Maria *and then became Carnival's* Carnivale, *and then shortly afterward by Union-Castle's* Transvaal Castle, *later renamed* S. A. Vaal *and finally rebuilt for cruising as the* Festivale. *Within a decade the Company turned to brand new tonnage, the* Tropicale *of 1981, the* Holiday *of 1985 and finally at least two 48,000-tonners, the* Celebration *and* Jubilee, *for 1986-87.* (Everett Viez Collection.)

Above *The last of the Blue Riband holders, the* United States *was laid up quite near to her birthplace, at Norfolk, Virginia, in the autumn of 1969. With much of her transatlantic clientele gone, her operations deep into the red and with the lingering threats of damaging American seamen's strikes also in the offing, she soon became the subject of considerable rumour for reactivation. One of the most logical possibilities has been, of course, to sail again but as a tropical cruiseship. Sold in 1979 to Seattle-based interests, the plans to rebuild and restore the 990-ft ship have lagged. One of the more recent proposals has been to tow her to Hamburg for general conversion and then to complete the fitting out task in some US yard. If successful and kept to at least one schedule, the* United States *might be sailing again by 1987—with an all-white hull, topside swimming pools, an upper-deck joggers' course, saunas and discos, and appearances in warm weather ports. In the scene above, dating from 26 November 1968, the* United States *is arriving at the Newport News Shipyard for her annual overhaul. In this photograph the Home Lines'* Oceanic *is in dock, undergoing similar treatment.* (Newport News Shipbuilding & Drydock Company.)

Left *Continuing as one of the most popular short-distance cruise runs, the passage between New York and Bermuda has included several generations of ships. Among the more recent, added in the spring of 1982, Home Lines—long one of the most popular firms in the American cruise industry—introduced the 33,000-ton* Atlantic. (Home Lines.)

Above *Many older liners continue to attain high profits in the cruise trades. Eastern Cruise Lines'* Emerald Seas, *used on the very popular three- and four-day runs between Miami and the Bahamas, has had an exceptionally diverse background and the distinction of having been refitted more than any other equivalent passenger ship. She began her sailing career in 1944, as the American wartime transport* General Wilds P. Richardson. *In 1948-49, she was converted for commercial passenger service, for the American Export Lines as their* Laguardia. *Briefly reused as a trooper, she later became the Hawaiian cruiseship* Leilani. *In 1960-62, she was rebuilt for the American President Lines as the* President Roosevelt *and then, a decade later, became the* Atlantis *for the Chandris Line. Her sixth life, as the* Emerald Seas, *began in 1972.* (Everett Viez Collection.)

Right *Another historic cruiseship of recent years has been the* Franca C, *owned by Italy's Costa Line. Originally built in 1914 as the American freighter* Medina, *she was converted to a passenger ship for emigrants in 1948. Some years later, after passing into Costa ownership, she was thoroughly rebuilt and re-engined for cruising. In the late sixties, while used in Caribbean cruising out of San Juan, she was linked to the first air-sea package tours ever offered with a cruise company. Highly successful, this soon spread to almost all firms. When finally retired in the late seventies, at nearly 65 years of age, the* Franca C *did, in fact, find further buyers. She has been sailing ever since as the missionary-style floating 'book fair'* Doulos, *travelling to underprivileged areas throughout the world.* (Operation Mobilization.)

Left *While well-known companies such as the Hamburg American Line, Cunard and P&O once could claim to having the largest ocean liner fleets of all, this title passed to the Soviet Union by the mid seventies. Their deep-sea passenger ships then numbered over three dozen. While owned by the Ministry of Shipping in Moscow, they are, in fact, less often used by their owners, but instead chartered to European, Australian, Canadian and even American firms for luxury cruising. While often using discount passage rates and therefore becoming quite successful, their revenues in highly sought Western currencies then find their way back to the Homeland. The* Feodor Shalyapin, *the onetime Cunarder* Ivernia *and later* Franconia, *is shown berthed at Lisbon during a two-week cruise for London's CTC Lines.* (Luis Miguel Correia.)

Right *While the Soviets have acquired a number of 'second-hand ships', such as the aforementioned* Feodor Shalyapin *as well as the* Maksim Gorky, *at the left and the former West German* Hamburg, *they have also built a considerable fleet of brand new ships. Eighteen small liners, all of about 4,500 tons, were constructed in the late fifties. A larger class of 20,000-tonners followed in the mid sixties. Other series of ships, often in as many as half a dozen in each group, were built in the seventies and early eighties.* (Luis Miguel Correia.)

Above *Greece's Chandris Lines and their affiliate, Chandris Cruises, developed a considerable cruiseship fleet of older liners, mostly former American or British. All of them ran extensive schedules of cruise voyages, from two-weeks out of Southampton to the Canaries and West Africa, to Mediterranean sailings from Venice and Piraeus, South Pacific trips from Sydney and in North American waters, from Boston, New York, Miami and San Juan. The largest of all, the 34,500-ton* Australis, *was the former* America *of the United States Lines. The near-sisters* Ellinis *and* Britanis *came from another American shipper, the Matson Line, and were formerly the* Lurline *and* Matsonia. *The* Amerikanis, *perhaps one of their most extensive transformations, was the former Union-Castle* Kenya Castle. *(Luis Miguel Correia.)*

Right *After a very rich and colourful history on the North Atlantic, with early three- and four-stackers, Blue Riband holders, steerage ships and even several of the largest liners ever built, the union of the Hamburg American Line and North German Lloyd, as the Hapag-Lloyd, suspended their transocean voyages in 1971. Thereafter, the company concentrated, using a single liner, in diverse cruising. A decade later, they added their first brand new passenger ship since the late thirties, the 33,500-ton* Europa. *An exceptionally beautiful ship, with space for as few as 600 passengers, she travels on an annual schedule of varied voyages, from a week in the Baltic to nearly four months around the world.* (Luis Miguel Correia.)

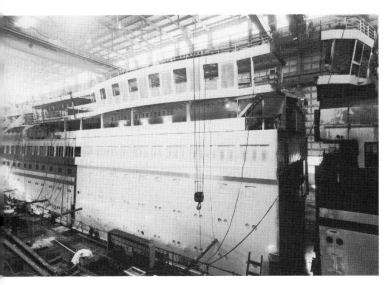

In the late seventies, just after a slump in the cruise industry and then prompted by a steady revival, many companies were at first reluctant to add brand new tonnage when pressed for additional berths. Consequently, several ships were 'jumboized', taken in hand by their builders and had specially built mid-sections added to the existing ship. With the additional cabins, public rooms and upper deck spaces, over 400 extra passengers could be carried. among those so treated in the early eighties were the Royal Caribbean Lines' sisterships Song of Norway and Nordic Prince, *the latter being shown during this transformation at her builder's yard at Helsinki.* (Wartsila Shipyards.)

Inspired by several earlier attempts, the Royal Viking Lines—which maintains one of the most de luxe cruise operations afloat—followed suit with their trio of sisterships, *the* Royal Viking Sea (*shown here*), Royal Viking Sky *and the* Royal Viking Star. *Their capacities, during shipyard alterations at Bremerhaven, were increased from 600 to 900 passengers.* (Hapag-Lloyd Shipyards.)

Theme cruising, particularly in the United States, has become especially important and popular. There have been musical cruises, beauty and fitness cruises, golf cruises, gardening cruises, nostalgic cruises and even murder mystery cruises. In January 1985, Cunard's Queen Elizabeth 2 set off for the Caribbean on a voyage with an unusual theme, a trivial pursuit cruise, based on the board game of that name. The voyage was a sell-out.

In the scene left, at Southampton, the QE2 is being repainted, returning to a black colouring in 1983 after a year's trial with an unsuccessful light grey. (Southern Newspapers Limited.)

In the tradition of earlier days at Southampton, when the likes of the Majestic *and* Leviathan, *and later the* Queen Mary *and* Normandie *rivalled one another for the prized distinction of 'world's largest liner', the greatest giants of the mid eighties met in the summer of 1985. The 70,200-ton* Norway, *the largest of all cruiseships, is sailing off for a Scandinavian cruise while the second largest, the 67,100-ton* Queen Elizabeth 2, *is still at dock.* (Southern Newspapers Limited.)

In a matter of months during 1984, three of the world's largest, finest and most expensive cruiseships came into service: Holland America's 33,800-ton Noordam *in April; Sitmar's 46,200-ton* Fairsky *in May; and then P&O-Princess' 44,300-ton* Royal Princess *November. All were assigned to the booming North American West Coast market, summers to Alaska and winters to the Mexican Riviera and occasionally farther afield through Panama and into the Caribbean.* (Holland America Cruises.)

Finnish-built, at the Wartsila Yards at Helsinki, P&O's Royal Princess *is nearly as large as the Company's earlier flagship, the* Canberra *(berthed in the distance in this view at Southampton). While flying the British colours and having been named by the Princess of Wales in an official dockside ceremony, the 760-footer will most likely not return to home waters for some time. Her operational base is in America, from both San Francisco and Los Angeles. Like almost all cruiseliners in today's cost-conscious, highly competitive industry, officers and crew members are relayed to and from the ships by aircraft. Similarly, drydocking is done in local yards. Those early day crossings for annual maintenance and crew 'rest and relaxation' are almost vanished completely.* (Southern Newspapers Limited.)

Left *Contrasting to the veneers, fireplaces, carved ceilings and oversized soft chairs of yesteryear, the International Lounge aboard the* Royal Princess *reflects indeed the liner's advertising title, 'the first cruiseship of the 21st century'.* (Wartsila Shipyards.)

Below left *Friendliness, informality and all of these blended with a near never-ending list of activities are the essences of the modern, highly successful cruiseship. The Riviera Club is a very spacious bar-lounge aboard the* Royal Princess. (Wartsila Shipyards.)

Above right *The North American cruise industry has grown to a £3 billion ($4 billion) level. However, most cruise companies admit that less than ten per cent of the potential market share has ever been tapped. Consequently, as new, highly sophisticated and more competitive liners are delivered, the firms must examine thoroughly ways and means of attracting new generations of ocean liner passengers.*

This rather unusual photograph of the starboard side of the Greek liner America *was taken while she was laid up at New York in the summer of 1978.* (Fred Rodriguez.)

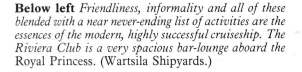

Right *Cruise companies must also seek new, more attractive destinations for their ships. Repeat passengers want different itineraries. While the Caribbean, Mexico, Alaska, Scandinavia and the Aegean remain popular, the future schedules may well show stronger emphasis in such areas as the South Pacific, South America, the Red Sea, the Antarctic and even far northward, to the Arctic.*

In this view a crewman attends to necessary maintenance on the Cunard Countess, *berthed at San Juan, Puerto Rico.* (Cunard Line.)

In these pages, we have seen some of the giants, the record breakers, the speed queens and Blue Riband holders, the big three- and four-stackers and the grey-veiled wartime troopers. There have also been the more distant passenger ships, serving the far-off outposts of an earlier era, and then the final fleet on the old, established North Atlantic route. The conclusion is with the new generation of white-hulled cruiseships, the floating fun palaces of today's ocean liner industry. However, while so much has changed, particularly the essence of the business from pure transport to pure leisure, some aspects have indeed remained the same. Among these, a quiet moment from a deckchair, peeping through a ship's rail and on to the magic of shimmering sea is still an extraordinary experience. Getting there is still half the fun! (Barry Winiker.)

Bibliography

Bonsor, N. R. P. *North Atlantic Seaway.* Prescot, Lancashire: T. Stephenson & Sons Limited, 1955.

Braynard, Frank O. *Leviathan: Story of the World's Greatest Ship* (Volumes 1-6). New York, 1972-83.

Braynard, Frank O. *Lives of the Liners.* New York: Cornell Maritime Press, 1947.

Braynard, Frank O. & Miller, William H. *Fifty Famous Liners.* Cambridge: Patrick Stephens Limited, 1982.

Brinnin, John Malcolm. *The Sway of the Grand Saloon.* New York: Delacorte Press, 1971.

Bunker, John G. *Harbor & Haven: An Illustrated History of the Port of New York.* Woodland Hills, California: Windsor Publications, 1979.

Crowdy, Michael (editor). *Marine News* (journal, 1964-85). Kendal, Cumbria: World Ship Society.

Dunn, Laurence. *Famous Liners of the Past: Belfast Built.* London: Adlard Coles Limited, 1964.

Dunn, Laurence. *Passenger Liners.* Southampton: Adlard Coles Limited, 1961; revised edition, 1965.

Eisele, Peter (editor). *Steamboat Bill* (journal, 1966-85). New York: Steamship Historical Society of America Inc.

Kludas, Arnold. *Great Passenger Ships of the World*, Volumes 1-5. Cambridge: Patrick Stephens Limited, 1972-76.

Kludas, Arnold. *Passenger Ships & Cruise Liners of the World.* Herford, West Germany: Koehlers Verlagsgesellschaft GmbH, 1983.

Maxtone-Graham, John. *The Only Way To Cross.* Cambridge: Patrick Stephens Limited, 1983.

Miller, William H. *The Great Luxury Liners 1927-1954.* New York: Dover Publications Inc, 1981.

Miller, William H. *The First Great Ocean Liners in Photographs 1897-1927.* New York: Dover Publications Inc, 1984.

Miller, William H. *The Fabulous Interiors of the Great Luxury Liners.* New York: Dover Publications Inc, 1985.

Miller, William H. *Transatlantic Liners 1945-80.* Newton Abbot, Devon: David & Charles Ltd, 1981.

Miller, William H. *Transatlantic Liners at War: The Story of the Cunard Queens.* Newton Abbot, Devon: David & Charles Ltd, 1985.

Miller, William H. *The Last Atlantic Liners.* London: Conway Maritime Press, 1984.

Padfield, Peter. *Beneath the Houseflag of the P&O.* London: Hutchinson & Company Limited, 1981.

Scull, Penrose. *Great Ships Around the World.* New York: Ziff-Davis Publishing Company, 1960.

Shaum, John H. Jr. & Flayhart, William III. *Majesty at Sea.* Cambridge: Patrick Stephens Limited, 1981.

Smith, Eugene W. *Passenger Ships of the World Past & Present.* Boston: George H. Dean Company, 1963.

Williams, David L. & De Kerbrech, Richard P. *Damned by Destiny.* Brighton, Sussex: Teredo Books Ltd, 1982.

Index

Great Passenger Ships of the World Volumes 1–6

Great Passenger Ships . . . to an island nation, steeped in a sea-faring tradition, the phrase offers not only the romance and excitement of ocean travel, but of travel in the Grand Style. This highly acclaimed series of books presents the details of that style, giving precise information on all passenger ships of 10,000 GT and over built from 1858 right up to 1985.

Volume 1: 1858–1912 includes technical detail, dates, lines of service and brief comments on items of interest for over 200 ships from the *Great Eastern* to the *Olympic* and *Titanic*.

Volume 2: 1913–1923 covers a period which saw the construction of the largest ships to date, the turbulent years of the First World War, and increased competition from other nations for traditional shipping routes.

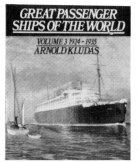

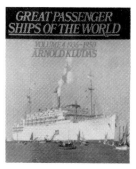

Volume 3: 1924–1935 embraces the introduction of superliners such as *Normandie* and *Queen Mary* — both of which won the coveted Blue Riband award — built in the lull between the two world wars.

Volume 4: 1936–1950, years of devastation and recovery! Details the many war emergency vessels constructed, new civilian ships, and the use of passenger liners as troopships.

Volume 5: 1951–1976. An era of dramatic change sees shipbuilding drastically reduced due to the growth of airline travel, a rapid rise in the number of car ferries built — and the production of outstandingly beautiful modern liners such as the *QE2*, *Canberra* and *Oriana*.

Volume 6: 1977–1986 gives the final fate of ships mentioned in volumes 1–5, subsequent careers of all appropriate vessels still in service and details of all new vessels of over 10,000 GT built since 1976.

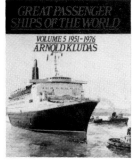

GREAT PASSENGER SHIPS OF THE WORLD, VOLUMES 1–6
by Arnold Kludas. Classic works of reference for the enthusiast.